ASSISTED REPRODUCTION: THE COMPLETE GUIDE TO HAVING A BABY WITH THE HELP OF A THIRD PARTY

ASSISTED REPRODUCTION: THE COMPLETE GUIDE TO HAVING A BABY WITH THE HELP OF A THIRD PARTY

Theresa M. Erickson, Attorney and Counselor at Law
Specializing Exclusively in Reproductive Law

With Maryann Lathus, Director of Conceptual Options, LLC.

iUniverse, Inc.
New York Lincoln Shanghai

ASSISTED REPRODUCTION: THE COMPLETE GUIDE TO
HAVING A BABY WITH THE HELP OF A THIRD PARTY

iUniverse books may be ordered through booksellers or by contacting:

iUniverse
2021 Pine Lake Road, Suite 100
Lincoln, NE 68512
www.iuniverse.com
1-800-Authors (1-800-288-4677)

ISBN: 0-595-34319-8

Printed in the United States of America

Table of Contents

Foreword

The world of assisted reproduction has forced our society to confront issues, questions and scenarios that were barely imaginable just 50 years ago. In fact, that is why this is a book that needs to be read by anyone considering or having to deal with surrogacy, egg donation, sperm donation or embryo donation—not because I have all of the answers, or even all of the questions, but because this is a complicated area that needs guidance. Actually, when I first became involved in Third Party Reproduction, the field itself was just developing and somewhat in its infancy stages. Yet, as medical technology advances with great speed, surrogacy and egg donation are now readily being discussed in the media on both popular sitcoms and news magazines.

Speaking of the media, it is so disheartening to see a news story or a press release regarding someone's fight to overcome infertility and how it destroyed their health for so many years. Often, the information that the media releases lacks the complete truth and is often misleading. Most importantly, it is one-sided. I know this to be true with any media coverage. They write what sells—and anything salacious sells news. Unfortunately, telling only half of this story can be all too misleading and often misguides those who are already experiencing heightened emotions and who have a deep fear of never having a child. To assume that any journalist's story does not include their own personal moral beliefs is sadly incorrect. The best advice is to read each media story as an opening for further research. Do not assume that the writer has even a remote working knowledge of the subject matter. Remember, everyone has an opinion. Seek out those that have something deeper to provide for your own success.

Actually, I first discovered egg donation during law school when I was reading a magazine article about a young woman who wanted to help another couple have a child while earning about $1,000. I was immediately drawn to these couples who so desperately wanted a child, and I began my own search by looking through the phone book for doctors who practiced in this field. I was matched immediately, and my donation resulted in triplets! I became so excited about what I had been involved in that I wanted to help more people have a family. Eventually, I realized that as a lawyer I could help even more people by practicing in this new and specialized area of law. It is through this dedication and my sister's own battle with her fertility that I narrowed my practice and my passion to exclusively Third Party Assisted Reproduction.

To be sure, this book is just a starting point for anyone considering having a baby through Third Party Assisted Reproduction. This guide, in a sense, can be used as a "roadmap" on your journey to having the child you have always wanted. Remember, no one ever expects that they will have to use a third party in their quest to have a child; however, you can empower yourself by knowing the facts, knowing the laws, and knowing the advantages and disadvantages of each before you commit yourself to just one choice. In fact, although this book does not cover adoption, everyone must remember that it is still a very viable option that cannot be overlooked in one's desire for a child. There are many children all over the world that need to be adopted by a loving family.

So, use this guide to help you see what lies before you as you begin this journey; and, remember, to stay positive and optimistic!

Theresa M. Erickson
San Diego
October 2004

Acknowledgements

There are so many people that have touched our lives while working in this field. In fact, we would like each and every client, egg donor, surrogate and embryo donor know that they hold a very special place in our hearts.

Specifically, we would like to thank the physicians that make this possible each and every day, as well as the psychologists and attorneys that make our team complete in every way. We would also like to thank all of the members of our staff, George, Jenn, Megan, Loren, and John, who have put up with our daily ranting and raving as this project reached it completion. And, we cannot forget our husbands and our children—John, Megan, Elijah, Dan, Andrea, Jacob and Sam—we could not have done it without you!

Chapter 1

Facing Infertility as a Team

With the recent increase of negative stories surrounding surrogacy and egg donation, one might be led to believe that there is a backlash brewing against these forms of creating one's family. That is exactly why it is important for those of us involved in this specialized field to continue to educate those considering surrogacy and egg donation, as well as those who will be touched by it in some way. Most important, we must promote that surrogacy and egg donation is not an adventure that one travels alone; instead, it should be seen as a journey that must include both an "experienced crew and passengers" alike.

Considering surrogacy can certainly be an emotionally daunting task for anyone. You must not only face your own inability to carry a child; you must also face the fact that someone else will be carrying your child for nine long months without you being present each and every second of the day. Furthermore, it is that someone that you will need to understand and learn to trust with your most precious cargo. Even with egg donation, you must learn to face that the child you (or your surrogate) will be carrying is not genetically your own. Despite this fact, it is still a child who will be cherished by you and your loved ones all the same.

In our experience, the majority of surrogate and egg donation arrangements that do not work out or that fail at some point along the way, involve either independent (those arranged without the use of an agency) or even unadvised situations (those arranged without the use of an attorney). Despite the financial considerations that go along with these arrangements, Intended Parents must

1

protect themselves, as well as their Surrogates and Egg Donors, by working together with a team of professionals who can guide them as they begin and continue their most wonderful journey.

We certainly believe that this book is essential to have throughout the process, as well as in the beginning to help you deal with the first important question—where do I start? Our job is to be your guide as you face certain issues, ethical dilemmas and the questions that you never thought that you would have when you first decided to have a child. In fact, this book is the first of its kind because it will help you select the right members of your team, guide you through the legal red tape, select the agency that is right for you and one that will do their job as agreed, and help you make the right decisions that will affect your future child, as well as your pocketbook.

Now, one of the most important first steps is to get your own thoughts in order. If you are still unsure of how to proceed or where to look, ask questions, questions and more questions. "No question is stupid unless you do not ask it!" And, no one wants to end up stupid in this sort of situation. You can either begin with your doctor, your attorney, your psychologist, your best friend, your family, or your local Resolve chapter. Just be aware that there is always someone to listen and talk with you who either deals with this daily or has gone through this situation themselves. You are not alone!

Next, you need to find the right team players. Just as in the NBA, a team will not make it to the Finals unless the right players are there to advise you and help you along the way. This is not an endeavor that one should travel alone. Just as you would not try to climb Mount Everest without the proper training, supplies and guide; surrogacy and egg donation is not something you want to turn to without the proper help and guidance from those who are experienced, dedicated and professional.

Of course, you will need a dedicated, warm and compassionate IVF physician who can provide you with the appropriate medical advice for your situation. Your physician must have a reliable, caring staff, an on-site coordinator, an on-site counselor, an experienced and qualified embryologist, as well as a well-equipped surgery center. Also, verify your physician's credentials and check what their percentages of births are in relation to the type of procedures that they perform. Their percentages are not the sole indicators of their success; however, they are a good measurement tool.[1]

You should next consider an attorney who specializes in the field of reproductive law. He or she should be experienced, dedicated and caring, not just an attorney who believes that they can draft up this sort of agreement with only

---

1. www.cdc.gov/reproductivehealth/art.htm

minimal guidance. The attorney's office staff must also be caring and compassionate because they are often the ones whom you will call when you are depressed, angry, upset or just need to talk.

Furthermore, your attorney should be one who can both advise you and counsel you in this very delicate, yet legally confusing, area of your life. Certainly, an attorney who specializes in egg donation, embryo donation, surrogacy (both traditional and gestational), insurance issues, trust administration and even adoption is the best to handle your dream of a child so that you will not have to hire a new attorney/counselor for each step in this process. Most important, you must remember that the legal portion of your surrogacy and/or egg donation arrangement is usually the most inexpensive cost that you will incur; however, it is certainly one of the <u>most important aspects of your journey</u>.

Equally, an agency is another aspect of your well-arranged team that should not be overlooked or chosen without some research. The agency should be well-versed, compassionate and willing to work with you throughout your questions, concerns and financial arrangements. The agency should be the <u>member of the team</u> that schedules all of the appointments, arranges counseling, handles any issues that arise in your arrangement, and handles all of the endless footwork. Speak with the agencies that you are interested in, speak with their directors and visit with them if possible.

Finally, once you have done all of your homework and selected the members of your team, you will be ready to move forward to the starting line. Nothing in this field is guaranteed; however, with the right time, the right attitude and thorough preparation, you can rest assured that you have done everything that you can to make your journey as smooth and error free as possible. Certainly, you may encounter a few bumps in the road along the way; however, this book will continue to be there as a guide as you find that you have additional questions, concerns or issues.

Chapter 2

Deciding Which Family Building Option is Best for You

When It Feels As If You Have No More Options

Although deciding which option is best for you is often the hardest decision, this is a decision that needs to be made by you and your partner (if applicable) only! Your physician's recommendation <u>is important</u>; however, you are the only one who can decide what is best for you and your family.

A. <u>Gestational/Traditional Carriers (Surrogates)</u>—This is an option for men without female partners or women who are unable to carry a pregnancy to term. Either the woman's own egg is used or that of an egg donor depending upon the situation.

B. <u>Egg Donation</u>—This is a wonderful option for men without female partners or for women who have poor ovarian response or poor egg quality. In fact, women who use egg donation often have very high pregnancy rates.

C. <u>Sperm Donation</u>—This is a successful option for women without male partners or for those couples where the man has low/no sperm or where they have chosen not to utilize ICSI.

D. <u>Embryo Donation</u>—This is a somewhat new option that has a lot of religious backing due to the option that life begins at conception. Some programs consider the process as a donation, while others consider the process as an adoption that involves a home study.

E. <u>Adoption</u>—There are many forms that adoption takes—international, domestic, agency, attorney or adoption facilitator. Although this book does not touch on adoption, it is certainly an option that is viable for many. The emotional issues are just as complex as with other family formation issues; however, those who have experienced adoption feel that there is nothing better.

F. <u>Child-Free Living</u>—Although child-free living is not a very accepted option by many in society, this is still an option for many that cannot be overlooked. If you feel that this is an option that you want to consider, there are many resources available to help you in that decision, including counselors who will help in making the right decision for you and your family.

This book will go into detail about each one of these options (except for adoption and child-free living) so you can determine what is right for you and your family building.

Chapter 3

Ethics and ART

My Friends and Family Are Asking Me What?

Certainly, we can not move any further into this book without discussing the topic of ethics and ART[2]. As most are aware, the topic of ethics and assisted reproduction is something that has been debated for years and will continue for years to come. In fact, we cannot even attempt to put an emphasis on ethics in this book since it would take an entire book to consider each and every issue. Yet, one important issue for anyone to consider as they determine the best family building option for them is disclosure. Should you tell your family/friends and should you even tell the child? The answer to that question is a very personal one that may take you many years, and maybe many therapists, to determine. But, it is an aspect that you should consider at some point. This, of course, is not a question that anyone can answer for you, but it is one that needs to be confronted.

Furthermore, egg donation, sperm donation, embryo donation and surrogacy bring with them an entire series of ethical issues for us to consider. For example, who monitors the clinics, the physicians, the attorneys and the agencies? Currently, there is no pending legislation either nationally or state-wide; however, the ASRM and each state's bar association monitors the doctors and lawyers. As

---

2.   ART—Assisted Reproductive Technology

for the agencies involved, you really need to do your homework to ensure that they are following proper screening and are following legal procedures as well.

In addition, informed consents in this field can be very confusing for the patient due to the technical knowledge that is often required to understand the procedures. Individuals need to ensure that they understand the risks, the benefits, and the legal implications in the documents that they are signing. In fact, in a California case titled <u>Kristine Renee H. v. Lisa Ann. R.</u>[3], the Supreme Court has the unfortunate obligation to sort out a lesbian couple's custody dispute when one partner signed an egg donation consent and the other signed a surrogacy consent. If you are not aware of what you are signing, there can be years of complications to deal with as this couple is currently doing.

One other issue that has been hotly debated is whether ART is doing more harm than good. In fact, are more people being helped by ART than being harmed? Will the use of PGD[4] cause genetic discrimination and create a "master race" of biologically superior humans? Of course, this is only the tip of the iceberg, but it is certainly something to consider when weighing your options.

---

3. 120 Cal.App.4th 143 [2004]

4. Pre-implantation Genetic Diagnosis

Chapter 4

Surrogacy

When You Need Someone to
Carry Your Baby for You—

What is Surrogacy?

Gestational Surrogacy (In Vitro Fertilization)—In this option, the recipient family creates embryos that are transferred to the surrogate mother. The surrogate mother then gestates the child but maintains no genetic link. The eggs can be provided by either the recipient mother or by an egg donor. The client family then petitions the court to change the birth certificate. In some states this is done before the birth, while other states require it done after the birth. This modified birth certificate reflects the correct parentage of the child. Also referred to as GS.

Traditional Surrogacy (Artificial Insemination)—In this option, the surrogate mother donates her egg. The partner or a donor provides the sperm that is used to fertilize the egg inside of the womb and create a child. The surrogate mother gestates the child and has a genetic link to the child. The client family them completes a step-parent adoption or the client family petitions the court to change the birth certificate so that the client wife/partner becomes the legal mother of the child. Also referred to as TS.

8

What to Consider When Considering a Gestational Carrier—

This Will Cost Me How Much?

A. Financial—$35,000 to $100,000

1. Medical expenses (up to $20,000)

2. Agency costs (up to $20,000)—ensure you understand what services you are paying for. If you choose to find a surrogate on your own and manage the arrangement, understand that it takes a lot of time and energy to manage the logistical, emotional and financial aspects

3. Legal expenses $6000 to $8000

4. Carrier costs $12000 to $35000 plus potential additional expenses for lost wages, childcare, housekeeping, medical costs and travel expenses.

B. Emotional—Are you ready to move on from own fertility treatments? How do you feel about someone else carrying your child? Are you and your partner both ready to do this? How will you explain this to the child and others?

C. Legal—Make certain that you find an attorney that specializes in reproductive law to help you understand the state laws that govern the arrangement. Ask how your name will be placed on the baby's birth certificate. Properly drafted agreements can serve as a map for a great relationship.

D. Medical—How will you and the carrier handle medical concerns such as issues during the pregnancy, amniocentesis, multiple gestation, and potential medical risks?

Once you decide that you are ready to move forward, make certain that you learn from others, consider the lessons from this book, contact Resolve or other organizations for guidance, talk to a counselor and/or physician, and research on the internet (although with caution).

Selection of Your Surrogate—

Where Do I Begin?

The following is a list of minimum criteria that should be followed. Women who meet the following guidelines should only be considered for further screening:

Ages of 23–39 (33 for Traditional Surrogates), with some exceptions

Capable of making an informed consent

Good pregnancy history to include no miscarriages, no pre-term deliveries, no stillborn, and a maximum number of cesarean sections

Willing and capable to follow strict medical guidelines

Given birth to at least one child and active in parenting her child/children

Supportive husband/partner if married or in committed relationship

Free of sexually-transmitted diseases

Non-smoker/Non-user of illegal drugs/substances

Not alcohol-dependent or prone to excessive alcohol use

Not currently on public financial assistance

Financially stable and independent

No prior convictions

Adequate social/emotional support for self & her family throughout process

*Most important—where she is located and where she will give birth

Screening of Your Surrogate—

What Should I Be Looking For?

As important as the selection of your carrier is the screening of your carrier by yourself, your doctor and, most importantly, by a licensed therapist/psychologist who can speak freely with your surrogate about the following issues:

Start with a criminal and financial background check

Discuss her motivations

Discuss her expectations concerning her contact/relationship with the Intended Parents

Discuss the outcome of this arrangement

Discuss her personal and moral positions—regarding amniocentesis and abortion/selective reduction. Remember, this issue must be discussed in length since <u>Roe v. Wade</u>[5] still applies to surrogates. You cannot force your surrogate to abort or not to abort through the help of the courts; however, the surrogate may be found in breach of the agreement if this occurs.

Discuss her religious preference and how that may affect your arrangement

Ascertain her mental health

Ascertain the likelihood of any power struggles between the parties

Ascertain the best form of closure for the surrogate and her family

Most experts recommend that the parents, as well as the surrogate and donor, seek professional counseling before proceeding with third party reproduction because of the many psychological issues surrounding these processes. In fact, this step is always required by physicians and cannot be and should not be waived, unless it has been completed previously within the last six to twelve months. Essentially, this step supports a positive arrangement, as does the creation of a thoroughly drafted agreement between the parties.

---

5.   410 U.S. 113 (1973)

Then, once this preliminary screening is complete, the process should not end. You need to continue to build your team and develop a referral network so that you and your surrogate have the ability to freely discuss any issues and potential problems with each other or other members of your team. Both the Intended Parents and the Surrogate need to understand that counseling is an ongoing process that should be available and open to both parties as the arrangement progresses.

Furthermore, while it is important to listen to your gut when dealing with third party arrangements, you must also not obsess over the arrangement. More often than not, obsessing can merely sabotage the arrangement before it even begins. Use education to get over your fear of moving forward and ensure that all of the steps described in this book have been followed.

To The Intended Parents of Surrogate—

Some Basic Instructions to Get Started

Although there are no federal, state or private agencies that track surrogate births, it is estimated that about 22,000 babies have been born through surrogacy in the United States since the mid-1970s.

Couples and surrogates enter into surrogacy arrangements for many different reasons and from different legal perspectives than those in adoptive situations. Likely the most common question many parents are asking themselves when starting down this road is, "How on earth did we get to this point?" Because, let's be honest, little girls and boys do not dream of having another person, other than mommy, carry their own children. However, when we arrive at the point of considering surrogacy as an option, the end result should be the same—acceptance. Suffice to say that every couple has a different story or road that brought them to this decision. Whether it is secondary infertility, a second marriage, birth defects, injury, unexplained infertility, or the lack of a female partner in the relationship, every person must truly accept surrogacy as a viable option, without regrets. There is no turning back the clock, or changing how you got here, so allow yourself time to realize and accept this as your reality and destiny.

Facing the loss of one's fertility is said to be likened to accepting the loss or death of a loved one. There is a grieving process everyone must go through in order to come to the final step. If any of the steps are missed or skipped over, it is difficult to ever come to terms and peace with your loss. Allowing yourself the proper time to grieve before moving forward is most often recommended. This is not to say that every person needs the same amount of time. Some couples are truly ready the day that their physician informs then that this is the recommended path, while some couples will never quite have closure over their loss.

What makes this particularly difficult to many couples is that both partners will not come to terms at the same time. This almost always a huge strain on any relationship. Having to accept the feelings of one another, as well as being patient while your partner continues to grieve, is very difficult—especially when all you can think of is getting started on creating your child. Infertility is extremely challenging to many marriages and relationships, but it is possible to move toward a greater level in your relationship than you ever thought possible and to realize the depth of your love for each other to make it through this together.

We often recommend counseling to many couples, and we have been given tremendous feedback as to how helpful it was to meet with someone, even if only once. Psychologists and counselors that specialize in third party reproduction and family counseling provide remarkable and invaluable insight on what you are experiencing. They can help to advise you in selecting a surrogate, as well as what type of relationship is going to be best for everyone in the long run. A number of the psychologists in this field have become parents via surrogacy or egg donation themselves, so they truly know first hand what you are feeling and experiencing.

Vulnerability and exploitation are also issues for the Intended Parents who need to make certain that their funds are handled through an escrow account or an attorney's trust account since you can never be assured that the agency will handle your funds either responsibly or legally. In fact, this is a common problem that no one wants to talk about.

Ultimately, the Intended Parents are still responsible for reimbursing their surrogate or egg donor even if the agency has misappropriated the funds or disappeared off the face of the earth. I have encountered many situations where the agency has either run off with the funds or went out of business with no further address. And, often Intended Parents do not have the energy or the funds to prosecute these cases. In fact, since these agencies are not licensed by any state, they are often only monitored by themselves, unless they are owned and/or operated by an attorney or a physician. The State of California, for example, does ensure that escrow agents[6] and attorneys as trust account holders are regulated and scrutinized in order to ensure that you and your money is protected. However, intended parents must have the time and money to actively prosecute these cases.

Furthermore, always use an attorney for your contracts. It is essential that you use an attorney that is experienced in this field of law since the issues in this field are not something any family law attorney can handle. The laws in this field are rapidly changing, and you must have an attorney that is familiar with these developments and their implications on your arrangement. In addition, you may think that you can use a sample agreement from a friend or one that you found online; however, I have reviewed numerous agreements that were created in this manner. I have found that five times out of ten, this online agreement does not do what you had planned or is weak against any potential legal challenge.

In all actuality, the contract process itself can also be seen as a screening tool for both the intended parents and the Surrogate since one party can learn a lot about another party from how they compromise or fail to compromise. But, do

---

6. California Financial Code §17700, 17701 and 17200

remember that this is not a fail safe tool, especially since attorneys and their egos are also involved.

To be sure, the need to be a parent is so strong that the risks involved legally are not going to stop most from moving forward. As a matter of fact, the laws surrounding surrogacy in most states is so fluid that one cannot completely be protected. All that you and your attorney can do is minimize the risk involved because these risks (to include insurance, human behavior and the law) cannot be eliminated.

Of course, be careful of agencies that charge for template surrogacy contracts or physicians who hand you template contracts for your use. Legal representation is a must when dealing with your future children. Their template may seem to fit your situation, but it may not be applicable. Are you willing to take that chance? In addition, it should cause concern when the agency (or even the physician) wants to keep you from obtaining legal representation.

For example, there is one agency that charges for a template surrogacy/egg donation contract in addition to their agency fee. While this may first appear to save you some money, this is actually illegal even if the agency discloses that they are not attorneys. Furthermore, this particular agency also states the following verbatim and is illegal, as well as dishonest:

"This agencies responsibilities are as follows:

1. Prepare a standard form of contract between the Recipients and Egg Donor and review the Contract with the parties prior to signature to confirm it properly reflects the agreement of the parties and the terms of the egg donation arrangement and to provide an explanation of its terms. By signature hereto, the Recipients acknowledge that no employee of is an attorney and, therefore, cannot advise Recipients or Donor with respect to the advisability of signing the Contract.

2. Recipients acknowledge that they may elect to have an attorney of their choice prepare and/or advise them with respect to a Contract between them and their chosen Donor, at their expense, and that no adjustment will be made by [this agency] to the Legal Contract Fee. Furthermore, Recipients acknowledge that the Donor they select may request representation by independent legal counsel and that, in such event, Recipients will pay the reasonable cost of Donor's counsel through the agency's Client Trust Account."

The example above is only one case in point of how Intended Parents can be misguided by those that are supposed to help them. Also be wary of the agencies that may be only in business to make money and not help you in your journey.

Of course, Intended Mothers should also consider breastfeeding of their child delivered by a surrogate. In fact, it can help with bonding with your child. The La

Leche League can be instrumental in helping you determine if this is an option for you. They can also help counsel you so that you will not be afraid to fail.

Finally, the location of your surrogate and where she is going to give birth should be an important aspect that cannot be overlooked. While there are surrogates available in every state, you cannot assume that they can move forward as your surrogate. The implications of the laws of her state (or the lack thereof) are instrumental in determining if your surrogacy arrangement will ultimately be successful or not and whether you can obtain the rights to your child without the delays and legal aspects of an adoption. If you select the right state for the location of your surrogate, you will not have to worry about your surrogate changing her mind and the potential for sharing custody with your surrogate. And, while you may be concerned that your surrogate may change her mind and recant the agreement with you, historically, it is actually three times more likely that you, as the Intended Parents, will recant your agreement than your surrogate.[7] That sort of statistic should definitely make you rest assured.

Remember, surrogacy is a very emotional issue for many people. Some believe that it is baby selling, while others feel that the surrogate is renting her womb. In fact, there is also the notion that this is a personal service contract which cannot be defined by a written or enforceable agreement. Yet, while keeping these issues in mind, you can determine how to best handle your own arrangement and determine the state where you want to proceed.

Finally, if you reside outside of the United States and intend to take your child back to your country, ensure that your reproductive attorney is familiar with the laws of your country in particular. Certain countries, including France, Italy and Japan, are tightening up their laws regarding surrogacy.

---

7.   Managing Legal Risk in the Assisted Reproductive Technologies Environment, Part II—"Keeping Out of the Sand Traps in Third Party Reproduction Cases," by Mark John and Sara M. Clay for ASRM Conference Papers

Insurance Coverage—

Beware! The Industry Motto is Still "Deny, Deny, Deny"

Do not blindly assume that your chosen surrogate's health insurance will cover your arrangement. In fact, it is prudent to have an experienced attorney review the policy before you move forward with any transfer or insemination. In the event that her insurance does not cover the surrogacy (or specifically does exclude surrogacy), your attorney can refer you to a specialized insurance broker who can determine the policy that is right for your needs.

Furthermore, it is always advisable to obtain another policy (despite the cost) due to the potential for insurance complications and costs if the surrogate's own policy does not cover. Of course, never consider trying to cover up a surrogacy at the hospital in order to have the insurance cover the pregnancy and delivery. We have seen far too many cases of insurance fraud that makes the wonderful joy of birth turn into a legal nightmare.

International Couples also need to verify insurance for their own coverage since coverage under the surrogate's policy ends at delivery. All Intended Parents are required to cover the child once birth occurs, which can be a problem if the child needs to go into neonatal intensive care. Remember, it is important to work with your attorney to ensure that you and your surrogate have adequate coverage in order to make your child's birth a smooth journey.

Estate Planning Documents—

Make That Will or Trust Now!

It is essential to ensure that your estate planning documents and/or wills are in place once your surrogate is confirmed pregnant. You will want to ensure that there is a guardian in place in the unlikely event that you pass away before the child is born (or even thereafter). Furthermore, make certain that your estate planning documents also discuss any issues regarding frozen sperm, eggs, or embryos that you may have in storage. It is important to deal with this issue now so that you can ensure that your wishes are carried out in the future.

To Surrogates and Their Families—

What Are We Getting Ourselves Into?

It is often said that surrogate mothers are angels, yet you are so much more. There is no price that can be placed on the gift you are providing. The gift of joy, the gift of love and the gift of a family that you helped create shows your dedication to helping others. In fact, the gift that you are providing is inconceivable to many. You create hope and life to so many parents that words cannot even describe your selflessness.

One important piece of advice that I always give to my new applicants is to be prepared for scrutiny. It is important to realize that not everyone will realize the beauty in what you are doing. A vast majority of society cannot grasp the concept of surrogacy and by preparing for those potential negative remarks, you can help deal with your own feelings during the process. Yet, the questions that you must most prepare for are those that are asked by parents at your child's school, your pharmacist, or even your favorite checker at the grocery store in your community. It is imperative that you, as well as your family, discuss what might be said and plan your response to questions such as, "how (or where) is your baby?," or "do you have a name picked out?" Planning a family meeting or role-playing discussions can best prepare everyone for open honest answers or a simple evasion.

And along with these questions and the negative remarks, a large part of what most surrogate mothers come up against is ignorance. Take for instance our own personal situation. You would think that doing what we do for a living would mean that our family members understand our career and position. Yet, although I have been personally affected by infertility and have been helping couples battle with their own problems for many years, some in our family still believe that surrogate mothers are "selling their babies." Whatever your particular case, generations and cultures present a variety of challenges with acceptance and comprehension. Being strong and rising up in spite of adversity is part of what makes a surrogate mother so special and unique.

A recent study conducted by the University of California, Irvine, suggests that a combination of variables attributes to a woman making the final decision to become a surrogate. It is so important that this study is published to educate society. It brings together the reasoning behind a surrogate's choice, and it will hopefully enlighten and enrich the perception that so many hold on the subject. This study so eloquently puts together the variables of charity; giving of oneself, financial gain, family values and the need to please and help others—all of which are necessary in the woman's final step toward pursuing surrogacy.

Yet, vulnerability and exploitation also exist for the surrogate and her family, not just the Intended Parents. For example, be wary of Intended Parents who do not want to place their funds with an escrow agency or an attorney. Make certain that your funds are handled through an escrow account or an attorney's trust account since you can never be assured that the agency will handle your funds either responsibly or legally. In fact, this is a common problem that no one wants to talk about.

Ultimately, the Intended Parents are still responsible for reimbursing you even if the agency has misappropriated the funds or disappeared off the face of the earth. And, often the surrogate feels sorry for the Intended Parents and/or does not have the energy or the funds to prosecute these cases, just as mentioned previously.

Furthermore, the surrogate (especially in California) has no rights to the child of the Intended Parents, even if she does not receive her reimbursement/compensation under the Surrogacy Agreement. This is the main reason why surrogates must also ensure that all rules are followed and corners are not cut at your expense. We all hope that everything will go smoothly, but that is not always the case.

Some additional problems for the surrogate include her Intended Parents and her agency not paying health care premiums and medical bills. In fact, a third time surrogate that I just counseled had suffered not once, but twice when her first agency took money from her and also assigned her a fictitious lawyer who never contacted her. It was the agency that was actually handling the contract on her behalf.

Then, her second problem occurred when her second agency failed to pay some medical bills, which later ended up in collections and ruined her credit for seven years. Apparently, she is an optimistic person since she really wanted to do this again under proper supervision; however, you must ensure that this does not happen to you and your family. Make certain that the agency is fair and will represent your interests and not just the interests of the Intended Parents who pay their fees.

Next, one of the most common questions asked of me by surrogate mothers once they start their journey is "What should I tell my children?" The answer varies greatly dependent upon the age of your children; however, the message is always the same. Your children need to understand that you are helping another mommy with her baby. You can present it as "holding her baby," or that "mommy's belly is like a nest for her baby," or even "that her belly is broken" and that you are helping.

However it is stated, they should understand clearly that you are <u>helping</u> someone. Children learn great lessons from us—lessons that we aren't even aware of teaching. If surrogacy is approached as a positive thing, then they will cue in on that. Often children will not understand completely the depth of what you have done for another couple, and more than likely they will not even grasp the magnitude of it until they start their own family.

Whatever the case, helping another human being should never be embarrassing or kept as a secret. Our children know much more than we give them credit for; and, if they perceive this baby as a family secret, then they will come to perceive it as taboo. If they are old enough to realize that there is a baby, then they should understand who this baby is for and why the baby will not be living with you once they are born.

This doesn't mean that your child will not come to you later and say "where is our baby?," and "why did you leave the baby at the hospital?" Children need confirmation from you that the baby is safe and happy and with his family. Reminding them of the story of how the parents found you and a willingness to repeat this story will often alleviate most concerns. Whatever the case, you are the center and focus of your child's understanding, and he or she will feed off of you for their security and comfort.

Which leads me to the next subject of how close should our families become? I personally feel that the best possible surrogacy arrangement is open and personal, however; this is not always possible due to geography, cultures, and other personal situations. It is very difficult to advise intended parents as to what is right and wrong, because it is almost impossible to get into their heads. In fact, for a woman to accept that another woman will take her place in the family and will carry forth the duty that she always dreamed of or promised to her husband in marriage is excruciating, to say the least.

Yet, every parent must come to term with this in their own way, and all we can do is to consult with them and provide them with the tools to carry forth with the best relationship that they know how. We impress upon the parents that a close relationship with their surrogate is the most psychologically healthy arrangement there can be; however; knowing what is best and getting there are often two separate issues.

Now let's say, for instance, that you are not afforded with the opportunity to be close to and open with your intended parents. Perhaps they live half-way around the world, or they are unable to openly make a connection with you. No matter what the case, this does not have to lend itself to feelings of regret, guilt, or negativity. Trying to keep yourself positive and honest about the subject is still the best thing you can do. Even explain to your own children how much the mommy and daddy of this baby wish that they could be with their baby, perhaps showing them a map of where they live. Explain how it breaks their heart to be so far from their baby. If the situation is not geography, then try to focus on how sad the mommy and daddy are that they miss their baby and that they are trying to be as strong as your family.

In addition, for your children to see these people as the baby's parents from day one, even if they are not present, makes the entire picture clearer for them along the way. To at least be able to have a picture or put a face to what they are told is the baby's mommy and daddy is often enough to satisfy their curiosity. I often tell my clients that seeing the intended parents holding the baby after the delivery helps to put everything into perspective.

Essentially, you are truly the pillar of this new family as well as your own, and there are an awful lot of people depending upon you for their happiness. Surrogacy takes a great deal of strength and commitment that most women do not have the ability to endure. The fact that you have taken the first steps toward becoming a surrogate mother shows how driven you are to give of yourself.

Legal Implications of Surrogacy—

Be Sure to Dot All of Your I's and Cross All of Your T's

NOTE: Understand that surrogacy involves the human experience and choice—control cannot be gained even with a complete legal contract in place.

Statistically, one out of every six couples will experience a fertility related problem during their lifetime. Fortunately, the courts in California provide the most favorable legal forum for surrogacy and egg donation for couples/individuals in California, the entire country and throughout the entire world, regardless of whether they have utilized their own egg/sperm, donated egg/sperm or donated embryos. All parties to a surrogacy (and egg donation) contract can be comfortable knowing that their intentions under their contracts will be upheld in the state.

Most importantly, a carefully structured agreement is necessary to ensure that the parties have resolved any possible issues, as well as any potential differences, before the surrogate becomes pregnant with the child of the intended parents. The agreement must protect both parties and ensure that not one party is left at a disadvantage.

Yet, once the surrogate becomes pregnant, it is important to notify your attorney so that the legal documents necessary to establish paternity and/or maternity are in place well before the birth of the child. Six months of gestation is a good rule of thumb to follow when deciding when to notify your attorney. Once the judgment to establish paternity and/or maternity are filed and executed by a Superior Court Judge (in the State of California), custody of your unborn child is awarded to the Intended Parents upon the birth of the child so long as the child is born in the State of California (within the limits of the jurisdiction of the Court's judgment). In this judgment, the Court orders the hospital to enter the names of the Intended Parents on the original birth certificate so that their relationship to the child is immediately recognized. This procedure eliminates the need for any adoption proceedings.

As far as traditional surrogacy is concerned, the risk carried by the Intended Parents is always considered to be greater than that of a gestational surrogate due to the fact that it could not be guaranteed that the child would be awarded to the Intended Parents if the surrogate attempts to assert her maternity (since she is essentially the egg donor and the carrier). However, it appears that this risk is not as great as it was in the past since arguably a recent California Court of Appeal decision has provided the same protections that exists in a gestational surrogate agreement to that in a traditional surrogacy situation.

The following excerpts from a gestational surrogacy agreement can further describe how surrogacy arrangements in California are the best forum for couples/individuals when deciding to create their family:

California Supreme Court Decision in Johnson v. Calvert[8] to Apply

While the undersigned are entering into this Agreement with the intention of being fully bound by its terms, the Parties have been informed and advised of the California Supreme Court decision in the case of Johnson v. Calvert and agree said decision applies to and governs this Agreement and the conduct of the Parties contemplated hereby. In Johnson v. Calvert, the California Supreme Court held that although the Uniform Parentage Act [9]recognizes both genetic consanguinity and giving birth as a means of establishing a mother and child relationship, when the two means do not coincide in one woman, she who intended to procreate the child—that is, she who intended to bring about the birth of a child that she intended to raise as her own—is the natural mother under California law. Further, in deciding the issue of maternity under the Uniform Parentage Act, the California Supreme Court felt free to take into account the parties' intentions, as expressed in the surrogacy contract, because in the view of the Court, the surrogacy contract was not, on its face, inconsistent with public policy.

California Court of Appeal Decision in Buzzanca v. Buzzanca[10] to Apply

The Parties further acknowledge that they have been informed and advised by their respective counsel of the recent California Court of Appeal decision In Re Marriage of Buzzanca and agree said decision also applies to and governs this Agreement and the conduct contemplated thereby. The court in Buzzanca held that the artificial insemination statute[11], which makes a husband the lawful father of a child unrelated to him, applies to both intended parents, husband and wife, who together have contracted with a surrogate, who agreed to the implantation of an embryo that consisted of egg and sperm that came from unidentified persons, and thus, the intended parents would be treated as natural parents. Furthermore, under the Uniform Parentage Act, the wife's parentage was not limited to giving birth or contributing genetically to the child.

---

8. 5 Cal.4th 84 (1993)

9. Family Codes Sections 7600, *et. seq.*

10. 61 Cal.App.4th 1410 (1998)

11. Family Code Section 7613

a. The <u>Buzzanca</u> holding goes on to further state that the forms of artificial reproduction in which intended parents have no biological relationship with the child does not result in legal parentlessness; such "adoption default" model is inconsistent with public policy that favors, whenever possible, the establishment of legal parenthood with the associated responsibility.

b. Although the <u>Buzzanca</u> case does seem to indicate that a stepparent adoption may no longer be required where there is any type of surrogacy contract, including both IVF and artificial insemination cases, certain courts may still require a stepparent adoption.

c. Whether or not an adoption is required, the Parties understand and agree that they will do all things necessary to assist in the legalizing of the parent/child relationship between the Intended Parents and the Child, as more fully set forth herein.

Most other states fall into one of four categories when surrogacy is involved:

A. <u>States where it is a crime to pay for surrogacy</u>—Arizona (ARIZ. REV. STAT. ANN. §25-218 (A)—all surrogacy contracts are void and unenforceable), Kentucky (KY. REV. STAT. ANN. §199.990—violation is a felony), Michigan (MICH. COMP. LAWS ANN. §722.857(2), .857—making it a felony to procure surrogacy agreements for compensation or to enter into surrogacy contracts with a minor or a mentally infirm woman), New Mexico, New York (N.Y. DOM. REL. LAW §123—imposes a felony for third parties who recruit or procure women to become surrogates and leveling a civil penalty upon those who enter into a surrogacy agreement; however, you can enter into an unpaid agreement in this state), Washington (WASH. REV. CODE. ANN. §26.26.250—you can enter into an unpaid agreement in this state, otherwise it is a gross misdemeanor), and Utah (UTAH. CODE. ANN. §76-7-204(1)(d)—makes surrogacy a misdemeanor);

B. <u>States where surrogacy agreements are unenforceable</u>—North Dakota (ND. CENT. CODE. §14-18-05—all surrogacy contracts are void and unenforceable), Nebraska (NEB. REV. STAT. §25-21, 200(1)), Indiana (IND. CODE. ANN. §31-8-2-1—all surrogacy contracts are void and unenforceable), Louisiana (LA. REV. STAT. ANN. §9:2713 (A)—all surrogacy contracts are void and unenforceable), District of Columbia (D.C. CODE. ANN. §16-402—accesses a civil penalty, and/or imprisonment, for personal involvement in, or assisting others, to enter into a surrogacy agreement. All surrogacy contracts are void and unenforceable), and Tennessee (TENN. CODE. ANN. §36-1-102 (46) (A)—all surrogacy contracts are void and unenforceable);

C. <u>States where they have laws that recognize surrogacy through legislation and/or case law</u>—California, Kentucky (prohibits payments and surrogacy programs), Massachusetts, Ohio, Oklahoma, Arkansas (ARK. CODE. ANN. §9-10-20(b)), Florida (FLA. STAT. ANN. §742.13, .15, .16), New Hampshire (NH. REV. STAT. ANN. §168-B), Nevada (NEV. REV. STAT. ANN. §126.045), Tennessee, Texas, Virginia (VA. CODE. ANN. §20-156) and West Virginia (W.VA. LAWS §48-4-16(e)(3)—all surrogacy contracts are void and unenforceable);

D. <u>The remaining states do not address surrogacy; therefore, your agreement and rights are uncertain.</u>

E. <u>As for the rest of the world</u>—commercial surrogacy is specifically banned in a number of countries: Switzerland, France, Greece, Israel (this country has recently legalized noncommercial surrogacy arrangements), Germany (which also bans egg donation), Spain, Britain, Italy, and Norway. In Sweden, the country has also banned the use of donated eggs or sperm. Furthermore, in Britain as of April of 2005, egg and sperm donors will lose their right to anonymity so that any child that they help produce can find out their identity at the age of 18 years.*

* <u>Note</u>: this information is an attempt to provide guidance regarding the important issues that egg donors, surrogates, embryo donors, sperm donors and Intended Parents should consider prior to entering into any agreement. This is not meant to replace representation by and consultation with medical professionals, mental health counselors or lawyers handling these arrangements. The serious nature of the legal rights of the parties in these agreements necessitates careful research and consideration prior to entering into any agreement. A carefully drafted agreement must detail consents and should outline the issues involved. Furthermore, the agreement must delineate the rights and responsibilities of all parties to the agreement. It is only through this process that the parties can be confident that a child born through third party assisted reproduction is free from legal conflict.

Chapter 5

Egg Donation

This is <u>Your</u> Baby!

Egg donation has slowly become an acceptable method by which to have a baby since the first child conceived from a donated egg was delivered by a woman with ovarian failure in 1983. This procedure involves the removal of eggs from a donor, and the transfer of those eggs into either the intended mother or a surrogate. These medical advances have provided infertile couples with the ability to have a child genetically related to one partner and one partner having the option of being the gestational carrier. In fact, developments in this field have provided hundreds of thousands of women (and men) the ability to carry a child when they have had premature ovarian failure, insufficient ovaries, abnormal eggs due to genetics or age, or ovarian failure due to chemotherapy/radiation.

What must be paramount to those individuals and couples utilizing egg donation is a program that provides them access to prominent physicians, reputable attorneys and specialized mental health care providers. Counseling by all three of the above-listed professionals is imperative for anyone considering egg donation, specifically in the areas of evaluating the risks involved in the required medical procedures and the legal ramifications of entering into an egg donation agreement by all of the parties. In fact, their consent must be voluntary and understanding of the procedures involved. Furthermore, the donor must also understand (prior to the commencement of the medical treatment) that she is waiving all parental rights that she may have or may have had over a child created by the use of her eggs.

Under current California law, a well-drafted agreement will give all parties the confidence that a child born through egg donation will be free of any legal conflict. Essentially, it is critical that the egg donor and her spouse relinquish their parental rights, and the agreement must be drafted in such a way to ensure that all parties understand and agree that any child born pursuant to this Agreement is considered the child of the intended parents. As far as the rest of the United States is concerned, only five states have passed legislation (at the time of the writing of this book) defining the status of children born by egg/embryo donation. Florida, Oklahoma, North Dakota, Texas and Virginia all have legislation that relieves an egg donor from all parental responsibility and rights and transfers them to the Recipient Intended Parents. Oklahoma is the only state listed above that does not recognize embryo donation.

In addition, a well-drafted agreement will specify that it is the egg donor's intent (and her spouse, if any) not to establish any form of parent-child relationship with any child born pursuant to this Agreement, as well as release the donor from any and all responsibilities regarding the care of the child. The Agreement will also address financial obligations of the Intended Parents, medical and psychological screening and the ownership and use of excess embryos. This is arguably the most important legal document to be executed by a couple or individual who want to have a child through egg donation since the courts have traditionally looked to the agreement to determine the intent of the parties.

In fact, the egg donor herself needs the protection of the agreement to ensure that she is released from any and all responsibilities regarding the caring of the child. As the Court in Johnson v. Calvert pointed out "any other result would unduly burden her with responsibilities she never contemplated and is directly contrary to her expectations." It is essentially the doctor's and her lawyer's responsibility to ensure that the donor and her spouse have sufficient information to understand the ramifications of the treatment, as well as the creation of any resulting child. It is critical that all disclosures be obtained in writing since the emotions involved in the arrangement are often very high.

Furthermore, Intended Parents themselves must ensure that their donor has received independent counsel and has signed an egg donation agreement, as well as all necessary consent forms provided by their physician, which memorializing parental rights and financial obligations. In addition, the agreement must address the short term and long term risks inherent in the egg donation process. Payments for medical insurance and legal fees are also generally assumed by the Intended Parents.

Intended Parents also need to be wary of egg donation agencies that charge for template egg donation contracts or physicians who hand you template contracts for your use. Legal representation is a must when dealing with your future children. Their template may seem to fit your situation, but it may not be applicable. Are you willing to take that chance? As I stated previously, it should cause you concern when the agency (or even the physician) wants to keep you from obtaining legal representation. Is the potential for future problems really worth the minimal savings of money?

As anyone in this field can attest, the number of egg donation programs has increased dramatically forcing Intended Parents to learn the hard way about which program is right for them and which program will provide the right donor with the right qualifications. For example, when selecting a donor program (whether through a physician or independent) ensure that the agency does not accept donors over the age of 29. While the ASRM[12] recommends working with donors over the age of 21, some do occasionally accept donors over the age of 19 if their current situation represents an increased maturity.

Furthermore, they must not accept any donors that have any family medical history of birth defects or genetic disorders, and the agency must strictly scrutinize any and all mental disorders within the immediate family through their medical and personal history profile. Finally, inquire whether the program interviews each donor and ask how many are actually accepted into the program. Be wary of those programs that remove information from a donor's application (besides private information for confidentiality) or accept each and every applicant.

Of course, one cannot consider egg donation without discussing the issue of anonymity. In the past egg donation has been based upon anonymity, secrecy and the lack of disclosure. However, when selecting an egg donor and an egg donation program you certainly need to consider is whether you want to remain anonymous or have an open relationship that can be defined by a telephone conversation or meeting in the agency's office up to knowing the other party's name and address. Intended Parents should explore these issues with their physician, as well as with a mental health care provider, which can help you discover your own issues and determine the path that you would like to take.

Most importantly, in the beginning you may want to locate an egg donation program that provides you the flexibility to determine the route that is best for you. Furthermore, this decision can also help you determine whether or not you are ready to make a commitment to parenting a child that is genetically related to only one or neither of you. It will also help you later determine what you want

---

12. American Society of Reproductive Medicine

to tell your child and how much disclosure you are willing to make to the child, and even to your family and friends. Remember, there is no right answer. The only answer to this question is something that you determine on your own or with the help of a mental health care provider that best fits you and your family.

What to Consider When Considering Egg Donation—

Again, the Money!

A. Financial—$15,000 to $25,000
1. Medical expenses (up to $20,000)
2. Agency costs (up to $8,000)—ensure you understand what services you are paying for. If you choose to find a donor on your own and manage the arrangement, remember that it takes a lot of time and energy to manage the logistical, emotional and financial aspects.
3. Legal expenses $600 to $1,500
4. Donor costs $3,000 to $20,000, plus potential expenses for medical costs and travel expenses.

B. Emotional—Are you ready to move on from own fertility treatments? How do you feel about someone else providing the genes of your child? Are you both ready to do this? How will you explain this to the child and others?

C. Legal—Make certain that you find an attorney that specializes in reproductive law to help you understand your state laws that govern the arrangement. Properly drafted agreements can serve as a map for a great donation.

D. Medical—How will you and the donor handle issues such as donation to science or to others?

As with surrogacy, once you decide that you are ready to move forward, make certain that you learn from others, consider the lessons from this book, contact Resolve or other organizations for guidance, talk to a counselor and/or physician, and research on the internet (although cautiously).

Gametes in the Marketplace—

What is Important to Me?

Extraordinary Donors...Do You Really Get What You Pay For?

Some agencies handle and arrange donor programs that focus on a donor's intellect, accomplishments, goals and ability (for example, extraordinary donors). However, what detractors must remember is that first and foremost, most parents do not believe that selecting a donor with a higher intelligence will guarantee them a genius child. Moreover, these parents are not trying to manipulate the gene pool of society—in fact, there are psychological reasons that are just as strong as the physiological and intellectual purpose.

At the point of parents having to accept donor egg as their last option for a child, there is a period of acceptance, followed by the loss of their dream and loss of a control of their own procreation that can not be explained. By selecting a donor that has similar qualities to oneself, including aspirations for a future and the drive to succeed, parents can look for more than just the physical. From our experience it seems to give parents back some control over a situation where they have almost none. Parents need to feel that they can give their child the best opportunity for a successful future, even if through the use of preferred genetic material.

One key aspect that we do attribute to extraordinary donors is their responsiveness to their physicians and coordinators, as well as their level of maturity. They are often more careful about their treatment and medication cycle and take their contract seriously. As pointed out previously, intended parents do understand that their child borne from donor egg that is considered "extraordinary" is guaranteed nothing more or nothing less than a child that is genetically their own. However, what they are finally guaranteed is hope and the ability to dream again. To dream of a future for the child they so desperately desire and to dream for their child to have the best opportunity possible is the least that we can offer intended parents, especially after every other hope and dream has been stripped away. There is not a single intended parent that would rather work with an extraordinary donor than to have their own genetic child. They are placed in the position to make this difficult decision by circumstances that are far beyond their control. Who are we to deny them this ounce of control they yearn so deeply for?

Egg Donor Selection—

What is Important to My Success?

Only those women who meet the following guidelines should be considered for further screening:

Between the ages of 21 and 34 with some exceptions

Family history free of genetically transmittable diseases, both physical and mental

Capable of making an informed consent about their donation

Willing and capable to follow strict medical guidelines

Free of sexually-transmitted diseases

Non-smoker/Non-user of illegal drugs/substances

Not alcohol-dependent or prone to excessive alcohol use

Not currently on public financial assistance

Financially stable and independent

Adequate social/emotional support throughout process

To the Intended Parents of Egg Donors—

Here are the Basics That You Need to Know

The moment of conception—the moment that has caused more controversy legally, ethically, and scientifically is one thing for certain—is an absolute miracle. For many women who cannot conceive a child because they produce few or no eggs or low quality embryos, this miracle becomes simply a dream or a reality to everyone but themselves. This is particularly common in women over the age of 40, where even with the vast scientific technology of IVF shows limited success. Additionally, women who have a genetic disease or a condition that they do not wish to pass on to their child, dream and hope for an answer—an answer with real hope.

In selecting and egg donation agency, you must look for one that offers a comprehensive egg donor program with a coordination team that has made many numerous donation cycles not only possible, but successful. They must also maintain a large number of <u>egg donors</u> who meet very <u>specific and stringent criteria</u>, and the agency must follow the most up to date guidelines and recommendations set forth by ASRM when screening and selecting donor applicants for their donor egg program. In fact, the most successful egg donation programs <u>only accept an approximate 50% of women who apply</u>. And, as stated previously, intended parents should have the option to choose from an anonymous, semi-anonymous, or known relationship with their donor.

For the intended parents, the agency should also not discriminate on the basis of medical need, household situation or personal lifestyle choices. The desire to have a child to raise and watch grow into a wonderful human being is innate in all of us. Furthermore, undergoing a donor cycle is not for every patient; it is extremely emotional and expensive. The process of acceptance prior to undergoing a donor cycle is similar to the loss of a loved one—one must grieve before they can move on.

Of course, the agency should also have worked with some of the most well-respected and knowledgeable experts in the field of reproduction. Numerous variables factor in to your chances for success, your age, the donor's response to the fertility medications, lab conditions, etc. The success rates of a donor cycle for a large number of infertility clinics and Reproductive Endocrinologists are currently at or above 70%.[13] However, because your fertility specialist and embryologist are the main key factor to your success, it is imperative that you do

---

13. SART results published by CDC

your homework, insist on references, and always, always, always—ask lots of questions.

The benefits of egg donation are insurmountable, and the ability to have a loved one or spouse provide half of the genetic make up of the embryo is something that can not be replaced after determining your need for a fertility assistant. Furthermore, the Intended Parents personally provide or control the prenatal environment—either through personally carrying the child created through egg donation or through the assistance of a gestational carrier, almost everything is within your control. You experience the pregnancy from early on through childbirth. Remember, these experiences are not always an option through adoption.

As for compensation, ASRM recommends that donors be compensated for their risk and time commitment, often penned as pain and suffering. Compensation generally varies from $4,000–$5,000 as an industry standard for a first time donor; however, there are donors that often request increased compensations due to their achievements and physical attributes. In fact, in 2000, ASRM released a report calling for a halt to the increasing "price" of human eggs. The organization determined that paying a donor $5,000 or more requires justification, while paying sums above $10,000 is simply inappropriate; however, the law itself is silent on the price to pay to an egg donor, and the price itself becomes an issue of supply and demand.

Upon selection, all donors must undergo additional screenings to include a complete medical and physical examination by your fertility physician, psychological screening, and laboratory screening for sexually transmitted diseases, hormonal tests, and any other lab screenings that may be requested for repeat by your physician. As not all physicians maintain identical protocols for their patients, it is only after they have reviewed your donor's file can the specific tests or screenings be determined.

To Egg Donor and Their Families—

Be Sure to Do You Homework!

As a donor, you are providing a wonderful gift to another woman. In fact, it is a beautiful example of women helping women; however, you need to make certain that your privacy and interests are also protected. For example, confidentiality on medical bills from the physician, hospital, or agency (to include your name and social security number) must be protected by them in the case of an anonymous donation.

Furthermore, you must ensure that your interests are protected by your attorney and your agency by insisting that any compensation for pain and suffering, as well as the funds for any medical bills, is placed into an escrow or trust account before you start your medications. This also includes your catastrophic insurance that will cover any and all medical bills resulting from complications from the egg donation procedure. And remember, your name should not go on any bills if at all possible since this runs the risks of either ruining your credit in the future or causing issues with your own insurance if you later have your own fertility problems.

Also ask questions of the agency or attorney to determine if you will be paid for travel time and expenses, whether your attorney's fees will be paid for by the Intended Parents, and whether you will be compensated if a cycle is cancelled before the retrieval itself. With these issues in mind, you can ensure that your own rights and responsibilities are protected in the event of any dispute. Of course, always ensure that you receive independent representation from your own attorney and that you sign a comprehensive agreement that is separate from the consent signed by you at the physician's office.

Remember, you are providing an amazing gift to someone who cannot have a child without your help, and always keep your focus on why you have been asked to help someone. Without the help of a donor, so many men and women would never be able to hear the words "Mom and Dad." While much of the process may feel more like a mere business arrangement (especially when you are dealing with the attorneys and the agency), it is so much more. Just realize that the contracts are there to protect you and the parents, as well as the child that will result.

In addition, your health and safety will remain paramount to the physician and the parents. Following the medical and legal instructions is important to your health, as well as a success outcome. Make certain that you take this seriously as this is the most important and emotional endeavor that any parent will ever embark upon.

A final consideration that must not be overlooked is the issue of taxation. Although this is discussed in length later in the book, it is important to determine whether or not the agency, attorney or physician that you are working with is going to send you a 1099 at the end of the year. Not only will this keep you in compliance with the IRS, it may also affect your decision regarding compensation for pain and suffering.

Genetic Testing—

This Affects Everyone

In the event you are requested to undergo genetic testing as an egg donor (or sperm donor or traditional surrogate), it is important to request that you are provided with the results of all genetic testing that is performed. In fact, your attorney should discuss whether or not to undergo genetic testing and its inherent implications, and they should advise you to seek medical guidance before making any firm decision. If you do choose to undergo the testing, you should request that you are provided the results (even if you do not want them). The intended parents should also be responsible for paying for your consultation with a genetic counselor so that you can understand the implications of your genetic characteristics.[14]

Finally, with the counseling by a genetic counselor, you can understand your genetic results and how they can affect your future (to include workplace and insurance discrimination), as well as the future of your other family members.

---

14. Hastings Center Report, Case Study on Genetic Testing in Assisted Reproduction with commentaries by Cynthia Fruchtman and Caroline Leiber, July-August 2001,

Donor Cycle Overview—

Timing and Medications

Through the use of birth control pills, your cycle will be coordinated with that of your donor. You may be administered suppression medications initially and start estrogen as your donor starts her stimulation medication. You and your donor also will need to have periodic blood tests and ultrasounds throughout the 2 to 3 weeks of treatment. This is not only to monitor the progress, but also to ensure the safety of both yourself and your donor by assessing hormone levels and your response to the administered medications.

On the day of the retrieval, the eggs will be fertilized and will be closely monitored in the lab. The length of time that the embryos will be allowed to grow in the lab is greatly determined by their quality and the preferred methods for success in your chosen lab/fertility center.

Progesterone injections commence on the day before the retrieval, continuing throughout the first 10–12 weeks of pregnancy. Dependent upon the quality of the embryos and your medical and pregnancy history, approximately two to four embryos are transferred into the uterus of the carrier (yourself or a surrogate). Any remaining embryos may then be transferred to cryogenics for storage for your future use. A pregnancy test is often scheduled between 10–12 days after the transfer.

If you are pregnant, your pregnancy will be monitored very closely by your fertility physician throughout the first trimester. After that time you will be released to an obstetrician that is often recommended by your physician.

In the event that you are not pregnant, you will discontinue the use of any medications and will wait for the onset of your period. After consulting with your physician, the best plan for proceeding will be determined. Provided that there are frozen embryos remaining, it is likely that you can attempt another cycle within a couple of months. Your physician's recommendation for proceeding forward after a failed cycle depends upon a number of factors, including but not limited to, their determination as to why the cycle failed.

Chapter 6

Sperm Donation

Certainly sperm donation has been around much longer than egg donation, yet it continues to be a viable option to many. Despite the many ways that insemination can occur, the simplest way is using the male partner's sperm and inserting it into his female partner's vagina. This is procedure is most often used in the event the physician needs to sort the sperm into categories of viability.

As far as the laws are concerned, there are not any laws that prohibit the use of insemination by anyone married or unmarried. Specifically, when a woman gives birth to a child that is created through insemination, the husband is the legal father without any legal procedures to follow, although there are some states that require the husband to consent to the insemination in writing. Furthermore, there are known donors and unknown donors, and it is the individual's or couple's decision where and how to obtain the sperm. Either way, a sperm donation agreement must be used in order to have a legally binding agreement in place to protect your rights to the child. In addition, it is important to obtain as much medical information about the unknown (and even known) donor before you no longer have that access. It is important for you and important for your child and their future.

As for home inseminations, while less costly, it is always advisable to undergo inseminations at a physician's office since some states only permit the woman's husband to be declared the legal father if the insemination was performed by a physician.

If you are selecting a sperm bank, ensure that the facility has guidelines for obtaining a complete medical history from the donor (including medical history that goes back four generations), tracking of the number of pregnancies per donor, limiting the number of pregnancies per donor, physical and blood tests on the donors, genetic and chromosomal analysis, and the freezing of sperm for a minimum of six months to allow for complete testing of the donor.

Finally, consider how you want the sperm bank you choose to handle anonymity. Some banks require that the donor's identity is revealed to the resulting children once they reach the age of majority.

Sample Sperm Donation fees:

1. Donor profiles—$10–15
2. Donor Audio interview—$20–25
3. Specimen freezing—$150–200
4. IUI Specimen—$250–300 per vial
5. Sperm wash—$150
6. Intrauterine Insemination—$150–250
7. Specimen Storage—$300 year
8. Overnight delivery $100

Chapter 7

Embryo Donation

Is This a Real Option for Me?

<u>What Is Embryo Donation and Where Are We Now?</u>—The Case for Donation and Adoption

It is actually estimated that there are well over 100,000 frozen embryos in storage in the United States alone. And, with the recent advances in ART and improved cryopreservation techniques, this technology has led to the wider use of frozen embryos for both donation and research. With that in mind, embryo donation still remains a comparatively new possibility that is just gaining ground as another viable option for those individuals and couples who have been desperately wishing for a child. In fact, it is often the only remaining viable alternative for those who have already been on the rollercoaster of infertility for many years and who have already invested significant amounts of time and money into their journey.

Although the number of available embryos may seem high, the actual number of embryos available to couples and individuals is really <u>much lower</u> since it is often a difficult decision to donate leftover embryos to someone else. In fact, many couples choose to destroy their remaining embryos or maintain them in the frozen state indefinitely since they are not willing to be contacted by any resulting child. On the other hand, the major motivations for the donation of one's embryos are usually to give the embryo a chance at life or to allow other infertile couples to have a child.

What the ideal solution for any person is, whether to thaw and destroy, donate to stem cell research or donate to another person, may be the biggest decision faced by those with embryos in storage—in fact, it is a decision that is highly ethical, morally, and emotionally charged. For example, full siblings may never know one another, and there is the issue of contacting genetic siblings and parents in the event of health and medical issues.

Legally, it is also often confusing since one school of thought believes it to be an adoption while others a donation—with those choosing adoption seeing the embryos as children awaiting their destiny. The description used is important since it has implications for both the pro-life and pro-choice movements. Whatever way you choose to view this possibility—every donor must certainly consider the following possibilities when making your decision:

a.) whether you will want the embryos for future siblings for any of your existing children;

b.) how you feel about the real possibility that there may be other children alive who are the result of your own genetic material or that of your partner and a donor; and,

c.) the pain of not knowing the result of your donation.

Once a couple has decided to donate their embryos, there is one additional legal issue that cannot be disregarded; this issue revolves around the agreement between the donor parents of the embryos and any egg or sperm donor that was involved in the creation of these embryos. Specifically, if an egg donor or sperm donor agreement is in place that spells out the donor parents cannot donate these embryos to another couple without his or her consent, then this must absolutely be followed in order to protect the rights of the recipient parents. It would be a tragedy to the recipient parents to have to deal with any litigation that may result if an egg donor discovered that the embryos from her donation were donated to another couple without her consent. Although the rights of the egg donor have already been terminated, this sort of dispute can be a very scary discovery for a recipient couple that has already given birth to their resulting child.

On the other hand, the options that are available to recipient couples and individuals are very few and far between once it has been determined that they need to move onto donor embryos. For example, you can sign up with a doctor's office that has a lengthy waiting list for available embryos, or you can contact an adoption agency such as the SnowFlakes Embryo Adoption Program, whereby the participants are required to follow the same requirements that exist for traditional adoption. The other options are to locate embryos independently online (which is absolutely not recommended without some guidance from a physician, lawyer or psychologist) or to sign up with a non-profit agency, such as Embryo Options, which provides the parties the option to tailor their arrangement to their own needs and desires, such as whether to have a relationship with the other party that is open, semi-anonymous or totally anonymous. Each of these programs are different in many aspects, and it is really a personal choice of any recipient couple or individual to choose the program that best fits their needs, whether religious, financial or otherwise.

In fact, once a couple or individual has reviewed the available programs, they need to be certain of a number of things before making a decision:

1.) Be aware of all financial requirements that are involved with these embryos, including but not limited to medications and clinic fees, if any, and whether the donors are requesting any fees in return;

2.) Ask questions about the program's own guidelines and protocol;

3.) Ask the program how donor parents and recipient parents are selected and matched. Discover if the parties have the option to turn down embryos that have been offered to them or not; and,

4.) Ensure that the recipients and their doctor are entitled to the embryo quality reports, the (redacted) medical records of the donors and the results of any successful pregnancies.

Yet, no matter if you are a donor or a recipient; the parties must follow a protocol that protects everyone, to include any resulting children. In fact, the parties must sign legal consents, have a counseling session with a psychologist or social worker, and undergo infectious disease screening. The purpose of counseling is to discuss issues such as disclosure to the child at an appropriate age—both for medical and social reasons.

From a legal standpoint, the legal system, nor the states' legislatures, has clarified the actual donation of embryos from one couple to another. However, the case of <u>Davis v. Davis</u>[15], as well as several others, has essentially given embryos the status of property when a dispute over the embryos arises out of a marital dissolution action. The courts chose to decide against "forced procreation," instead of providing the embryos with a higher (protected) status due to their ability to become life. In an effort to clarify the status of the embryos from the standpoint of donation, attorneys in this field have chosen to use this same argument to treat the embryos as the donation of genetic material, or property in a sense, from one couple to another much like egg donation.

Essentially, the lessons learned over the last decade have shown those attorneys practicing in this field that precise contract drafting is absolutely essential—your attorney must carefully scrutinize the contract terms since there is strong dicta

---

15. Tenn. 1992

favoring enforceability. Furthermore, the reimbursement of costs that may be requested by a donating couple must be considered very carefully before agreed upon by a recipient couple. Certainly, any additional medical testing required by the recipients' clinic, as well as any outstanding storage fees, are acceptable fees to be paid; however, anything additional can make the donation itself questionable. To be sure, the donation of embryos does not involve the same sort of pain and suffering associated with the donation of eggs; therefore, it is best to stay away any additional reimbursements that can be construed as the purchase and/or sale of embryos.

Finally, the success rates from the transfer of frozen embryos is certainly lower than that of a fresh embryo transfer, as is reported by ASRM; however, the availability of this option of donor embryos is certainly one that should be considered by everyone, donors and recipients alike. To donors, it is the chance to help others and provide life to their frozen embryos; while, to recipients, it is a viable alternative in their journey to creating their families—just remember to ensure that all parties, to include the resulting children, are protected.

As a final note: this option provides a partial solution to other people who have been dealing with an issue similar to yours—their infertility. In addition, it also helps solve another problem—the growing stockpile of abandoned embryos. Lessons learned over the decade have shown that precise contract drafting is an essential function for the attorney, who must carefully scrutinize contract terms since there is strong dicta favoring enforceability.

What to Consider When Considering Embryo Donation

Before considering embryo donation, you must look at the following differing opinions before making your decision:

Adoption is an excellent option for many couples. For some, however, embryo donation is a preferred alternative due to the fact that is often much less expensive than adoption because you do not have to pay for the expenses of the birth mother, and it is usually less complicated and less expensive than many alternative ART procedures since you do not have to pay the egg donor. Unlike adoption, one has a tremendous amount of medical information regarding the biological mother and the biological father of the donated embryos, and in turn, the identification of the biological parents can also help deter any uncertainty and future custody and legal issues.

Furthermore, the donor embryo recipient can protect and nurture the pregnancy minimizing the prenatal exposure to drugs and poor nutrition by carrying the embryo to term and experiencing the joy of birth. Privacy is also much greater in embryo donation than adoption.

On the other hand, embryo donation is possible because of ART; therefore, the individuals creating these embryos often have fertility problems themselves— thereby lowering your chances of success. In addition, your child can ultimately have full biological siblings in the world without their knowledge. Yet, the single most important issue against embryo donation certainly has to be their availability since there is very little selection or choice since so many are not willing to donate their embryos.

Chapter 8

Non-Traditional Families

Are You One and What Does That Mean to You?

For same sex couples, infertility is not an issue. In fact, you cannot get pregnant without using some form of family building discussed in this book. And now is a better time than ever with gay/lesbian relationships gaining acceptance around the world; a recent <u>Newsweek</u> poll discovered that 57% of adults polled felt that same sex couples were just as good as parents as heterosexual couples.

Some groups are even stating that the gay/lesbian community is in the middle of a full-fledged baby boom. Although some couples are finding co-parenting to be a popular option (whereby a lesbian woman or couple locates a gay male or couple to create a child and later co-parent), all other family building options such as surrogacy and egg donation are also gaining popularity in the community. This is especially true when couples do not want to deal with three or four parents, child support issues and visitation rights. In fact, the legal climate in states such as California has made non-traditional parenting a new and often risk-free option.

Gay and Lesbian couples who want to move forward through egg donation, sperm donation and/or surrogacy should first consult with a legal expert regarding donor and co-parenting agreements—to include the event of death/separation. Furthermore, the attorney must be knowledge of the current state of the law, such as in California where the State Supreme Court is set to review three cases involving lesbian couples as follows: <u>Kristine Renee H. v. Lisa Ann R.</u>[16], <u>Elisa B. v. Superior Court</u>[17], and <u>K.M. v. E.G.</u>[18]. Here, the State Supreme Court will be deciding whether the same-sex former partners of birth mothers have parental rights and responsibilities equal to similarly situated heterosexuals. Potential clients, as well as former clients who are concerned about their judgments already in place, should ensure the their attorney discusses the implications of these cases (if any), the implications of the revised California Domestic Partnership Law[19] that went into effect on January 1, 2005, and whether a pre-birth judgment is effective whether or not used in conjunction with a step-parent adoption.

Furthermore, do not assume that your physician is aware of the current state of the law in your state. In fact, we have come across a prominent physician in southern California who attempted to provide a lesbian couple with an egg donor consent and a gestational surrogacy consent in lieu of providing a more comprehensive document that would ensure that the true intentions of the couple were set forth. Certainly, all infertility clinics that offer services to gay and lesbian couples need to prepare documentation and resource materials with inclusive language and include that patient's partner in all discussions. Either way, be beware of your doctor's consent forms—or you may end up like the couple in the California case K.M v. E.G. where one signed an egg donation agreement and lost all rights to her partner's "child." Ultimately, the physician's informed consent process needs to include advising gay and lesbian couples to obtain legal advice as how to proceed.

Gay and Lesbian couples also need to beware of exploitation by any agencies, specifically due to the status in the community. Some agencies may charge more for their services since they specifically cater to gay and lesbian couples; however, all you need to do is locate an agency that is willing and has experience working with someone in your particular legal situation.

---

16. No. S126945

17. No. S125912

18. No. S125643

19. AB 205

Chapter 9

Choosing a Physician

This is Perhaps Your Single, Most Important Decision

Finding a good reproductive endocrinologist or fertility clinic can be a daunting task that you should take very seriously, especially since this is someone that you may be involved with for quite some time. In fact, we recommend that you create a list of physicians that are local and that come with recommendations from others. However, do not choose a doctor just because he/she may have gotten someone you know pregnant. Everyone and every situation is different; therefore, once you have your list, interview each physician and evaluate their staff. You should also evaluate their office and how well organized the office and its staff appears to be since there is nothing worse than selecting a physician/office and then later discovering that your cycle is being held off for several months because a test was forgotten or even misplaced.

Furthermore, when you interview these physicians, make certain that the physician is reputable and is on top of the developments in their field. Since fertility treatment is often a cash only industry, do not be misled by a "quack" that is out to make an easy dollar. Since the treatment that you will be undertaking is so emotional, you want to ensure that you select a physician whom you can trust and one whom you can talk to—make certain that his/her bedside manner is what you are looking for in a physician.

If you are someone who does not share their current situation with others, we suggest contacting ASRM, Resolve, the AIA[20] for referrals to those physicians in your area that are at the top of their field. You can also search various websites and join chat rooms/message boards; however, be wary of that information since you can never be certain of someone's motives or what their experience truly is. They may tell you that a doctor is horrendous because that physician was unable to get them pregnant; however, they may also be failing to tell you that they have certain medical issues that will forever preclude them from carrying a child to term.

You must also select a physician based on your own needs. Do you like to be hand-held, or do you like to be told the diagnosis in a business-like manner? Do you want a physician that speaks to you in medical terms or one that breaks things down so you can understand what is really happening to you? Do you want a physician who calls you back personally when it is an issue that demands one on one interaction? Do you despise waiting for hours in the waiting room? Does the physician communicate by email, fax and phone? What are the physician's statistics (and are they reported to the CDC[21] or SART[22]? How many egg retrievals and embryo transfers do they perform per week? Can you tour the lab and meet the embryologist? What are the embryologist's qualifications? Does the embryologist have a Ph.D. or are they an M.D.? Does the physician transfer freeze eggs? Does the physician transfer blastocysts and what are their criteria for doing so? What percentage of their patients experience Ovarian Hyperstimulation Syndrome? What are the physician's criteria for canceling an egg retrieval? Is the patient contacted before it is canceled if an egg donor is involved? What is the physician's protocol?

As for the statistics, review the physician's statistics that are particular for your situation/age group. Also, ask the physician how they determine their success/pregnancy rates. This is important to help you understand where you stand as a potential patient. In addition, ask if the success rate reflects chemical/clinical pregnancies or live-birth rates.

Another issue with success rates to consider is how liberal an admission policy the physician has. Some physicians will only work with patients that they know they can get pregnant, while there are a few others who work with those that are more difficult cases; this is certainly an aspect that can affect any clinics success rates that must be considered. Finally, once you have completed your physician

---

20. American Infertility Association

21. Centers for Disease Control

22. Society for Assisted Reproductive Technologies

interviews, compile a list of pros and cons. Hopefully, with that you should be able to narrow your list down to a physician that you can be comfortable with for your entire process.

Chapter 10

Consent Forms

How to Protect Yourself and Your Embryos—and Ultimately Your Children

Starting with the fertility scandal at the University of California (Irvine— UCI) and their Center for Reproductive Health in 1995 until today, many couples have been (albeit some remotely) concerned with the possession and disposition of their genetic material. It is true that eggs and embryos have been stolen and the deliberate switching of eggs and embryos has occurred between patients. In fact, former patients of that university have filed over 100 lawsuits.

What individuals and couples need to do to protect themselves is ensure that they become as informed as possible from the beginning to the end of their procedures. More importantly, in a field where the supply for eggs, embryos and surrogates has surpassed the demand for each, intended parents, surrogates and donors must be aware that some professionals involved in this field are not a trustworthy as they should be.

Be proactive in requesting consent forms that cover your particular procedure and situation. Make certain that the forms are clear by using signatures and initials on each and every page, not just check marks or x marks. The physician will provide you with many forms to sign authorizing consent, among other things; however, these forms do not establish parental rights. The forms are provided ultimately to protect the physician and their employees from any legal liability.

Furthermore, you must ensure that each and every party involved in your situation has signed a legal agreement delineating your rights and responsibilities. Make certain that you do not rely on your physician's legal agreements alone (also called informed consents). Make certain that your consent is clear and understood before you sign the agreement and make certain that you have this additional legal agreement between yourself and your donor, recipient and/or your surrogate.

In fact, with the recent news regarding the loss of embryos at clinics through negligence, you need to be certain of what will happen to your embryos at cryopreservation and what will happen to them if they cannot locate you at any time. Do not be flippant with signing these agreements in any way, no matter how rushed or emotionally drained you may feel.

Finally, ask questions, questions, and more questions. Make your physician provide you with the information that you are requesting without delay. Ensure that a count is done on your number of follicles, the number of eggs aspirated, the number of embryos transferred and the number of embryos frozen.

By maintaining a count of what you have, you can ensure that any mistakes are caught right away instead of like a woman in San Jose, California, who recently learned that she was implanted with the wrong embryo about ten months after she delivered her son. After years of litigation, she is still currently involved in a custody battle with the couple whose embryo she received. In this sort of case, the courts are forced to struggle with novel issues for determining parentage and custody using laws premised on outdated notions of maternity and the underlying assumptions about genetics, gender and race. Try to make sure that this does not happen to you.

Chapter 11

Choosing an Attorney

So, You Mean My Real Estate Attorney Cannot Help Me?

Finding a good reproductive law attorney can also be a daunting task that you should take very seriously since this is someone that you may be involved with for quite some time and that will be handling your rights as a parent. In fact, we recommend that you create a list of attorneys that you have found through your own research and from those that come with recommendations from others. Then, interview the attorney—do they provide a free consultation so that you can get to know them and their expertise? If not, you should think twice about hiring this attorney since their motivations may not be to help you in your journey.

Furthermore, ask for their fee structure—is it based on an hourly rate or a fixed rate? This is important in determining their affordability. Also, determine if the attorney is available for consultations during your arrangement in the event that you have questions or concerns. It is important to determine if they are willing to help in the event that you have a problem. Nothing is worse than having a legal problem that involves something as important as your child, and the attorney who drafted your agreement is unwilling to talk with you without a retainer in place.

Finally, make certain that the attorney you select is experienced and understands the law as it currently stands, as well as knowledge of recent developments. This is certainly not a time for you to hire a general family law attorney when your rights as a parent are involved. Also, think about issues such as: does the attorney seem sensitive to my feelings, does the attorney seem well-organized, does the attorney answer questions to your satisfaction and does the attorney openly discuss the financial and emotional risks involved?

Chapter 12

Cryopreservation

The freezing of human cells, whether sperm, eggs, or embryos is an important part of ART. Without cryopreservation many would not be able to freeze their embryos for future use or even freeze their eggs or sperm when one is facing chemotherapy.

One often overlooked, yet very important, aspect of cryopreservation is the drafting of a thorough and comprehensive agreement with your clinic that determines the cost, the length of preservation, ownership issues (to include divorce and death), the technique used to freeze the material, your preferences for disposal and/or donation, and what the clinic has in place in the event of disaster. In addition, if you are using donated material (sperm, egg, or embryo) ensure that your written agreement with the donor covers issues such as future use of frozen material and any restraints against destruction or donation.

Chapter 13

Pre-Implantation Genetic
Diagnosis (PGD)

A Medical Breakthrough and Dream Come True? Maybe,
Maybe Not

"Do we want to have a society where parents can flip through a DNA catalogue and design their own 'boutique baby'? Will we accept that it is perfectly reasonable to discriminate against people before they are born, or prevent them from being born, because we don't like their genes?"—Dean Hamer, Geneticist at the National Cancer Institute from "Remaking Eden" by Dr. Lee M. Silver.

For some couples, the dream for a family includes further concerns or fears, such as genetic disorders, that are very real and beyond the normal fear that all parents have for their unborn child. When one or more parent is a carrier of a genetic mutation, or they are aware of mutations present in within their family, the need for additional testing may be more than a convenience. It may very well be the only possibility or consideration for a child.

In fact, for years genetic disorders could only be detected during pregnancy using one of two methods: amniocentesis and chorionic villus sampling. Amniocentesis, which is done when the fetus is twelve to sixteen weeks old, consists of drawing a sample of the amniotic fluid from around the fetus and examining a floating cell from the fetus. Chorionic Villus sampling, on the other hand, involves taking a small sample of the placenta at an early stage of development and examining it in the laboratory. The problem that many have had to deal with these two procedures is that they can only be performed after conception and after significant fetal development. Therefore, if the analysis shows that the fetus is genetically defective, the intended parents are then faced with a decision of whether or not to terminate the pregnancy.

Now, intended parents, whose family history or genetic mutations placed them at risk had the options of accepting the risks listed above, considering the use of a donor, or choosing child-free living, have the procedure known as pre-implantation genetic diagnosis, or PGD, available to them in order to give them new hope for a healthy child. PGD allows researchers and embryologists to take a single celled biopsy of the couple's embryo and provide them invaluable information about the chromosomal composition of the embryo.

Whether the couple is experiencing infertility problems or not, IVF is a necessary part of PGD in order to then select those embryos determined healthy for implantation into the woman's uterus. The biopsy of the embryo at this stage does not damage the embryo or cause the resulting fetus to be "missing" something. While this is an understandable concern, it is not realistic and parents are advised to discuss the risks and benefits at great length with their fertility physician and embryologist before making the decision to proceed with PGD.

While there is never a guarantee on the health of your child, PGD offers some parents the next best thing. In fact, it has been characterized as the most important scientific discovery of the twentieth century; completely changing the course of the biological and biomedical sciences.

There are a number of specific mutations that can be tested through PGD. Some of the diseases that can be detected are Cystic fibrosis, Sickle cell anemia, Tay-Sachs, Spinal Musclar Atrophy, Huntington's disease, Hemophilia A and B, Fragile X, and numerous others. Additionally, many parents utilize PGD as a means of absolute sexing of the embryos for selection. Sex-selection is extremely useful in a variety of family situations, including those with X-linked disorders, family balancing, etc. Currently PGD is the only absolute in determining the sex of an embryo. There are other methods that are less invasive and carry far less risks; however, when the desire for one sex over another is absolutely necessary, PGD is currently the most viable option.

It is also worth mentioning that PGD in itself is very expensive and carries a number of risks to the embryo. At the time of printing this, the average cost of PGD is around $4,000–$5,000. That does not include the cost of the IVF procedure or the fees that go along with IVF. Additionally, the attrition rate for the embryos must be understood and accepted as a viable option for the procedure. For a number of parents the benefits outweigh the risks, especially when a known family genetic disorder exists. PGD should also result in only the best embryos being transferred into the uterus. Furthermore, the benefit of being able to transfer only the best, provides for less embryos being transferred, thereby reducing the risk of multiples in pregnancy.

Ethically, PGC avoids the trauma of having to terminate a pregnancy and enables couples to have a child with the assurances that the child will not be carrying on any genetic disease. Effectively, it allows intended parents to manipulate natural selection, which is causing geneticists and the rest of the world to consider whether or not this sort of intervention is moral. To be sure, intended parents can screen for genetic defects while potentially determining the entire genetic makeup of their unborn child. Could they choose a girl with fair skin and blonde hair, or can they choose a male child who is athletic?

Additionally, there are religious considerations since some groups consider the procedure to be the murder of a child since a cell that is removed could have conceivably developed into a fetus. Other groups also believe that a genetically fertilized egg, if allowed to mature and result in a live birth, may not produce a defect at all, or may not manifest any symptoms until the person is in his/her early thirties or forties by which time a cure could be developed.

To get a basic comprehension of the process of PGD, and to perhaps better evaluate one's options, it is important to understand the following: First, after the egg is retrieved from the mom or from an egg donor, the egg is immediately fertilized by sperm from the father or that of a sperm donor. Once the egg is fertilized, it begins to transform and becomes an embryo, carrying the DNA structure of the anticipated fetus. At this point a single-celled biopsy is can be conducted without effecting further development of the embryo. With the aid of a highly knowledgeable embryologist who is experienced in micromanipulation and biopsy, the cell is then evaluated. While awaiting the lab results on this cell structure, the remaining embryos are retained in the lab pending transfer instructions.

Due to the fact that the DNA evaluation takes a specified amount of time, the embryos in the lab are at potential risk. Embryos must be stable enough to "survive" in the lab for up to five days. This is difficult for some embryos, as those that have the potential for further growth in uteri, may still have difficulty in a lab medium. Understanding that the attrition rate can be and often is increased when forcing embryos to be maintained in the lab for additional time, can help you to determine if the pros outweigh the cons in your particular and very personal situation.

Chapter 14

Beginning the Process—A Checklist

Quite Lengthy Indeed—But Do Not Miss a Step!

What follows is a step-by-step guide to beginning the process of assisted reproduction. With the overwhelming number of techniques available today for couples/individuals to begin their families, many are unsure of where and how to begin. The following is an abbreviated step-by-step guide which can provide you with the information necessary to start the process. This guide is not meant to be a substitute for legal advice by an attorney. This is for information purposes only; each case must be assessed individually on a case-by-case basis in order to determine the proper steps you will need to follow.

A. <u>Speak with a reproductive law attorney</u>:

    ✓   You will need to seek advice to determine the status of surrogacy and egg donation in your state;

    ✓   The attorney will also consider the laws of both the state where the Intended Parents and Surrogate reside, as well as where the baby will be born;

✓ Currently, several states find surrogacy arrangements to be either unlawful or will find the agreements unenforceable.

B. Agency or Independent?

✓ Determine if you want to find your egg donor and/or surrogate independently or with the help of an agency;

✓ Currently, there are a number of surrogacy and egg donation programs that offer specialized services to couples/individuals considering assisted reproduction;

✓ Since there is little regulation in this field, it is very important for you to ascertain the type of services that these agencies will provide you for your money;

✓ For example, does the agency require their fees to be paid upfront before you have selected a surrogate or donor? What type of screening and protocol does the agency use in the selection or surrogates and donors? If the surrogate or donor does not pass medical or psychological screening, will they provide you with an additional surrogate or donor for no additional cost? These are just a few of the questions that you must begin to ask if you choose to use an agency;

✓ If you choose to go independent, will you be able to manage the relationship with your surrogate or donor? Will you be able to resolve any conflicts along the way yourself without the help of a neutral third party?

C. Determine Costs:

✓ Be certain that you are aware of the costs associated with the program you have selected;

✓ There may be hidden costs for additional cycles, lost wages, travel, child care, and unforeseen medical complications or consequences that are not spelled out in detail.

D. Informed Consent:

- ✓ Consult with any attorney to determine the risks and ramifications of executing an agreement with a doctor, agency, and/or clinic;

- ✓ Have your doctor explain to you and your surrogate/donor the medical procedures and risks involved with your particular treatment.

E. Confirm Insurance Coverage:

- ✓ Confirm that proper insurance coverage is in place for any catastrophic illness and/or medical consequences of the infertility procedures;

- ✓ Determine whether your policy, and/or that of the surrogate or donor, will cover any or all medications and infertility treatments;

- ✓ Many insurance companies are now denying medical maternity expenses to women serving as surrogates. Other insurance companies reserve the right to seek reimbursement from the Intended Parents for any maternity benefits paid on the surrogate's behalf;

- ✓ It is also imperative that the Intended Parents take the appropriate steps, in advance of birth, to have their child added to their own health insurance policy upon delivery.

F. Medical and Psychological Screenings:

- ✓ The Intended Parents, the Surrogate and her spouse, and the Egg Donor must complete a full medical examination which includes a variety of tests, including HIV;

- ✓ Psychological testing and evaluation of the Surrogate and Egg Donor is also very important. This screening should be done by licensed psychologists who perform a variety of tests to determine the suitability of the surrogate and donor for the Intended Parents.

G. Execute Legal Contracts:

✓ Have your attorney that will draft, negotiate and finalize legal agreements as needed with infertility specialists, agencies and third-party donors or surrogates;

✓ Ensure that your surrogate and/or egg donor is represented by competent, independent legal counsel, who must issue a legal clearance letter indicating that the surrogate (and her husband if she is married) and/or donor understands and appreciates the issues set forth in the contract, is proceeding with the arrangement voluntarily and without any coercion or undue influence;

✓ The parties must determine the following:

1. The financial responsibility of the parties

2. The legal responsibilities of the parties

3. Ensure that medical and psychological testing takes place

4. Address the ownership and disposition of any remaining embryos

5. Address what records must be maintained and by whom

6. Establish the parameters of acceptable conduct by the parties throughout the arrangement

7. Address insurance issues such as life, medical and disability insurance

8. Identify the mechanism to be utilized to finalize parental rights

9. Address issues of pre-natal testing and reduction

10. Establishment of a trust account

11. Compensation to be received by the Surrogate or Donor and what expenses will be reimbursed

12. Agreed upon contact, if any, the surrogate and/or donor will have with the child

✓ The parties must also discuss such decisions as the number of embryos to transfer and decisions relating to selective and fetal reduction, as well as guardianship instructions in the event of the demise of one or both Intended Parents;

✓ Additional issues to discuss include what the participants will tell their children, disposition of excess embryos, confidentiality issues, and the utilization of pre-natal testing, including pre-implantation genetic diagnosis and amniocentesis.

Chapter 15

Agency v. Independent & Online Matching

Consumer Beware!

If you are considering using an agency, think again. Alternatively, if you are considering going independent, think again. I know that this is confusing, but you must protect yourself no matter what. In fact, you want to ensure that you are prepared for either option.

The number one consideration that you need when choosing an agency, is that you need to find an agency that cares for you and your surrogate so that you are both able to focus on the baby. They need to treat the whole person—you and your surrogate! Make certain that you <u>THINK BEFORE YOU SIGN</u>! Are they only a matching service or are they more? Make certain that you know what you are obligating yourself to. Make certain that you sit down with the agency and "kick the tires" before you sign anything.

You should not choose an agency based upon their program fees or the fees that they pay their donors/surrogates. In fact, you need to discover what that agency will actually provide—do you need to sign an agreement before you choose a surrogate, do you have to handle the doctor's appointments, can the agency live up to their promises, and are those references for the agency real or contrived? Is the agency just a matching service, or do they provide support throughout the entire process for you and your surrogate/egg donor.

Furthermore, ensure that the agency will protect you and your surrogate/donor, not just themselves. In fact, I have seen many agencies that take advantage of intended parents' vulnerabilities, to include their status in society such as gay or single, by charging excessive fees and/or failing to provide each Intended Parent(s) with the flexibility to determine how they want the program to serve them.

If going independently, can you ensure your own privacy, is the surrogate or egg donor asking for a retainer fee in order to begin the process with you? Why is the surrogate or egg donor going independent? Is it to save you money or because they have already been turned down by agencies and physicians? Why is the donor or surrogate insisting on not hiring an attorney or agrees to do home inseminations?

You must be careful. In fact, cheaper does not always mean the best solution— saving money now can actually cost you more money in hidden costs and legal bills in order you receive your child. You always get what you pay for in this field as in any other. Remember, using a donor or surrogate or being a donor or surrogate is an emotional process that will need support from others, not just their treating physician.

I have one client in particular who decided that since she was a stay at home, she could handle her own surrogacy arrangement without an agency. In fact, she even located a wonderful caring surrogate on the internet. However, once she felt she had chosen the right surrogate; her story began to unravel since her surrogate began to demand a retainer for being her surrogate. Whether $1.000 or even $5,000, a retainer should not be paid since it is the intended parents who are already putting forth a lot of money and effort in order to begin the process.

I understand that some surrogates request a retainer to ensure that a particular intended parent(s) is serious and not merely "window shopping;" however, more people than not regret the payment of a retainer since the surrogate may disappear or may begin to ask for unreasonable provisions in her contract. And, once this retainer has been paid, many do not feel that they can turn back since so much has already been paid. I am not saying that you cannot pay your surrogate a retainer; however, I would recommend that she receives this retainer right after her first embryo transfer/insemination. Beware!

In fact, some intended parents become more worried about money than the fact that they are actually locating childcare for the next nine months. Don't you want to ensure that you have dotted all of your i's and crossed all of your t's? Will you just drop your child off at daycare once they are born without checking the provider's references, background, and criminal history? In fact, agencies protect both the surrogate and her Intended Parent(s). Agencies ensure that contracts are in place, escrow/trust accounts are funded, and psychological issues are tended to.

Even surrogates need to be careful. I have seen plenty of surrogates agree to no escrow account only to find out later that the Intended Parents do not have the money to pay them. Remember, the intended parents do not have to pay the surrogate in order to obtain their parental rights and their child in most circumstances, especially in California, because the contract has been determined to be separate from the establishment of parental rights. These are two separate cases—one in family court and one in civil court.

Note: anyone with enough time and energy can discover how to build a car or build a bomb (especially with the help of the internet), just as someone can locate a surrogate to act as their carrier while coordinating all of the details of the arrangement. However, you must remember that there are many potential problems awaiting those venturing into third party assisted reproduction. These problems inevitably arise just when you want to experience the joy of your child. Instead of foregoing the guidance of the professionals discussed in this book and opening yourself up to potential problems that await your limited knowledge, it is important to call on experts such as a doctor, an attorney and a mental health care professional for advice and guidance in this area. You may believe that you are saving money; however, you may be creating more problems and liabilities in the future.

The goal of surrogacy is one that needs guidance and protection in order to protect the child and the relationship of the parties. Do not be afraid that attorneys or counselors will only make things worse since a party that has had their own counsel cannot come back and say that they did not understand something. Finally, the greatest benefit of using professionals is having the ability to keep the business side separate from your personal relationship and experience—and isn't that what everyone wants?

Of course, the checklist below may help you in determining if a particular agency is for you and your family.

A. Does the agency ensure that an agreement is in place between the Intended Parents and the surrogate/donor?

B. Does the agency ensure that counseling is provided to the surrogate/donor and the Intended Parents?

C. Has the surrogate/donor been personally interviewed?

D. Has the surrogate/donor been provided with information regarding the procedures and any risks?

E.   Is the agency willing to provide donors that are anonymous, semi-anonymous or open depending on the needs of the parties?

F.   Does the agency limit the number of times of surrogate/donor has been used?

G.   Does the agency follow the guidelines set by the American Society for Reproductive Medicine regarding minimum requirements for screening, number of cycles per donor, compensation, and donor requirements?

H.   Does the agency reduce its fee for a subsequent donation/surrogacy?

I.   Does the agency offer financial plans that permit you to pay fees as they are incurred or at certain milestones?

J.   Does the agency have protocol in place in order to protect your privacy, as well as the privacy of your surrogate/donor?

K.   Does the donor/surrogate have independent counsel provided?

L.   What is the agencies protocol on maintaining records of the surrogates/donors?

M.   Does the agency have strict protocol for the selection of surrogates/donors? And, do they follow their own protocol?

N.   Does your physician's clinic offer egg donors? If so, what is their protocol?

As you may be aware, agencies often provide personalized searches for a donor, unlike many clinics; however, this can be costly. Certainly, agencies do provide a greater donor selection than physicians, although you do have the added backing of a respected clinic/physician. Either way, you must make certain the decision that works for you and your family.

Chapter 16

Tax Consequences

Is Uncle Sam Watching All of This? You Better Believe It!

I have reviewed several 1099-MISC forms that have been issued to donors, including myself, and I have found that the arguments for their issuance are unbalanced and uncorroborated since the description of egg donation as a "service" has yet to be defined by the IRS.

In fact, how can egg donation be a "service performed in one's trade or business by one who is not an employee?" Of course, the ASRM guideline merely suggests that doctors and clinics would be "wise" to issue a 1099; however, it is not clear as to why or what the case from the Federal Income Tax Appeals Division states. In fact, I could not even locate a case from this division that even discusses egg donation.

Now, it is my understanding that egg donation is neither a product (otherwise it would fall under an illegal enterprise due to the sale of human organs/tissue) nor a service since the egg donation process is clear that she is donating her eggs and not providing a service. In fact, it appears from the outset that egg donation, as sperm donation has been classified in the past, is not taxable due to the medical procedure that involves both pain and suffering during the course of hormone treatment, daily injections and an outpatient procedure at the completion of the cycle in order to retrieve the eggs. If this is the case, the amounts paid to the donor should fall under compensatory damages that one receives for physical injury or physical sickness and thereby fall under nontaxable income.[23]

Furthermore, it is my understanding that sperm donation has never been taxable to the men who choose to donate either once or even monthly. In this situation, a review of the standards that apply to men should also apply to women in order to alleviate any issues of gender discrimination/equal protection under the law.

Of course, if the IRS determines at some point in time that pain and suffering is not a factor in the donation of eggs, you should certainly consider the amount received by the donor as a gift from the recipient couple to the donor in return for the donation of her eggs. Certainly, if a donation exceeds the gifting limit of $10,000.00 per year per person, we may have another issue altogether.

As for the intended parents and taxation/ART, you would be wise to speak with a tax specialist since surrogate and donor expenses may be deductible if the services provided by those who are not medical professionals are necessary to treat the tax payer's condition[24]. With the rising costs involved in surrogacy and/or egg donation, the expense of a tax specialist will certainly be worth its weight in deductions.

---

23. IRS Publication 525
24. Internal Revenue Code Section 213

Conclusion

This is Only the Beginning!

The creation of your baby and the birth of your baby are two of the most emotionally charged and intimate processes in which you can participate...and that is when only two people are involved. Surrogacy, sperm donation, egg donation and embryo donation can add up to five more people into the mix; therefore, you have to be ready emotionally, financially and legally before deciding to move forward. However, do not let the fear of risk or the fear of disappointment stop you because once you hold your beautiful baby in your arms, it will all seem worth it. Good luck and take care.

Frequently Asked Questions

Remember, The Only Stupid Questions…

1. <u>What type of arrangements and relationships are available with most surrogacy and egg donor programs?</u>

Many agencies offer basic egg donor and surrogacy programs with a standard protocol and thereby a limited number of options for their clients. There are only a select few that exceed the standards of service and stand out as leaders in customer service and foremost providers in their industry. These leading agencies have the wherewithal to offer their clients with a wide range of resources to include a full coordination team that have successfully completed numerous IVF cycles. A formidable agency should maintain a large database of egg donors who meet very specific and stringent criteria. Similar rules should apply within their surrogacy programs, as numerous options provides for the greatest opportunity for your success and peace of mind. You should question your agency's options and programs in detail before committing. The type of arrangement and relationship that feels best for your particular situation is what you should be provided with, whether that is an open arrangement, with full identity disclosure, or complete anonymity. Surrogacy and egg donation is such a personal decision that you should be allowed to not only choose the setting that is best for you, but you need to also feel comfortable and supported in your decision.

2. <u>Then what type of arrangement is recommended?</u>

The textbook answer to this is that honesty is always the best policy. Having an open relationship with your surrogate mother is seen as providing your chosen surrogate with the best possible scenario for her and her family, as well as your unborn child. This provides you with the greatest opportunity to be a part of the pregnancy and experience, while insuring your surrogate feels supported and important as a necessary part of your life and your baby's life. However, it is important to understand that this is not an option for every family and in certain circumstances that it is acceptable to have a closed, or anonymous, arrangement with your surrogate. This is a very delicate matter to be addressed with your surrogate, and it is of utmost importance that your agency is familiar with and has the resources available to aide your surrogate mother through such an arrangement. Ongoing counseling and support for all parties is often recommended in this type of arrangement.

Similarly, with your donor arrangement, which in a majority of situations is totally anonymous, you should carefully scrutinize what is most preferential for your personal situation. If you are not certain as to whether or not you intend to tell your child at a later date that a donor was involved, be sure to gather as much information as possible from the beginning so that you do not close the door to your options down the road. I am not suggesting that you need to get to know your donor personally and exchange social security numbers; I am merely recommending having some basic answers for your child who may or may not have questions at some point in their life. To be able to tell him or her why you chose this particular donor and what traits you felt that she carried similar to your own is often told to be enough for closure.

Again, as with a surrogacy relationship, your donor situation is very specific to the individual. It is highly recommended that parents seek professional counseling advice to make a fully informed decision with the least regrets possible for the future.

3. What are the current success rates through third-party reproduction?

The success rates of a vast majority of professionals in this field are approximately at 70%. The best chance for every parent's success is by becoming fully informed on the success rates and experience of the clinic and/or physician you are considering. One of the highest recommended resources for comprehensive data is through the governmental organization SART, an organization that is completely dedicated to setting and improving the standards of assisted reproduction. SART collects and verifies data provided by member facilities that require accreditation. Their findings are published by the Center for Disease Control. Approximately 95% of the clinics in the United States are represented in their findings.

To review the most recent findings, visit the CDC internet site[25]. It is important to note that the findings reported by the CDC run about 2–3 years behind. Unfortunately with the technology of assisted reproduction, such data can be tremendously outdated; however, it is still an excellent resource for comparison data. After reviewing the SART findings, it is then recommended that you inquire about a particular clinic's current data during a consultation appointment to further evaluate their standings and updated statistics.

---

25. http://www.cdc.gov/reproductivehealth/art.htm

4. If I do not already have a fertility physician, where do I begin to locate the best clinic?

The ASRM is a great place to start. They will list physicians and clinics in your area, along with their credentials, etc. Another great resource is through local support groups. Contact organizations such as Resolve for a list of recommended providers in your area and talk to members about their experiences. Finally, speak with other professionals in the field. Ask attorneys and agencies for their recommendations as well.

5. What about other professionals services that I am considering? How do I know who is most reputable?

As with physicians, it is best to ask local chapters of support groups such as Resolve for a list of recommended professionals. Also, ask your physician for his or her recommendations. Because this is still a relatively small community, and because it takes a concerted effort by a number of individuals in the field to make a surrogacy and/or egg donation arrangement to be a success, most of the leading physicians, attorneys, and agencies have been working together for a number of years and will know first hand those that are most reputable and provide stellar service.

6. There is so much information out there regarding the "science" behind IVF, that I often feel ignorant to the terms and acronyms. There is a lot of discussion and debate regarding day 3 embryos, day 5 embryos, blastocyst embryos…What does this mean and how do I know what is best for my situation?

First of all, it is important not to feel ignorant. Yet, you can and will from time to time, but know that you are not alone. The most intelligent of individuals find themselves confused when presented with IVF and its options and procedures initially. It is important that your physician takes time and has a lot of patience with your situation. If you don't understand something, ask that it be explained again. If you are working with an agency, and/or an attorney, they should be more than happy to help with explaining and answering questions. While they cannot give medical advice, they certainly can explain terms and provide non-medical, but professional, recommendations.

So, back to the question at hand, your doctor and embryologist should provide you with detailed information about the quality of your embryos before transfer and then provide you with their recommendation. It is important to understand before selecting a clinic what their policy is regarding embryos and transfer. There are some clinics that only work with 3 day embryos (those are the ones that remain in the lab for 3 days after fertilization before being transferred into the uterus). While others feel strongly about advancing most or all to day 5, or what is also known as the blastocyst stage. For the most part, many physicians and embryologists work with a variety of culture media in the lab to hopefully maintain your embryos for up to 5 or even 6 days. The embryos are monitored very closely around the clock. When determined by the embryologist, the embryos are prepared for transfer. The advantage of working with blastocyst embryos is the reduction of multiple pregnancies. However, if the embryos stability is at risk at any stage prior, it will be recommended for transfer at that time. Your physician is always going to have your best interest in mind. He understands your immense desire or need for a healthy pregnancy and will make decisions and recommendations based on such.

7. <u>I am still trying to decide whether third-party reproduction is for me, or if adoption might be a better option?</u>

The benefits of egg donation and surrogacy are insurmountable. The ability to have a loved one or spouse provide half or all of the genetic makeup of the embryo is something that can not be replaced after determining your need for a fertility assistant. Furthermore, the Intended Parents personally provide or control a portion of the prenatal environment—either through personally carrying the child created through egg donation, or through the assistance of a gestational carrier. You experience the pregnancy from pre-conception on through childbirth. These experiences are rarely an option through adoption. Ultimately, the decision of whether to adopt or not is a very personal decision. While many well-meaning friends and family members will offer an argument either for or against adoption, only through your extensive research and personal preferences can you make the decision that is best and right for you.

8. <u>There are numerous references to "Extraordinary Egg Donors." What is an Extraordinary Egg Donor?</u>

Many agencies have donor programs that are termed anywhere from Exceptional to Extraordinary. For the most part, donors that participate or qualify for these programs must meet specific criteria through their educational achievements. It is important that you understand that the achievements of ones donor does not guarantee an increased intelligence from offspring. What we have specifically marked as a benefit for recipients to this program are donors that are responsible, driven and articulate in their achievements. These donors understand completely what is at stake and have proven themselves to be responsible and committed.

Furthermore, you should anticipate these donors to often request increased compensations above what is considered the industry standard. The American Fertility Society suggests that donors be compensated for their risk and time commitment, often penned as pain and suffering. Compensation generally starts at $5,000 for these donors and can often be much higher. It is highly recommended that some form of verification for achievements be provided for your review, such as a copy of transcripts, SAT, LSAT, GRE, or GMAT reports, or anything that you find acceptable for the stated accomplishment. Understanding that identifying information must first be removed, anything that is particularly important to you should always be provided to you for your own proof and piece of mind.

Determining if this is an important characteristic for your donor is equal to determining the physical characteristics that you deem important in your donor. It is again a personal decision. Many parents are often judged for their preference for an educated or accomplished donor. Preferring a smarter or more attractive donor will always be a subject for scrutiny in society.

Many outsiders (you know, those people who have never dealt with infertility, but have all of the advice in the world as to what is right, what is wrong, or what you should do) will never understand the feelings that are going through you mind or the thoughts on how to determine who is the best candidate for you. It is important to remind yourself that you are not a bad person for having specific preferences, and that in a perfect world; you would never be considering the selection of a genetic donor. This is not something that you opted for or ever dreamed would be your reality. Given the circumstances that have now been forced upon you, you need to take back a little from the fate you were handed. By sitting down and realizing that this is not what you wanted, but once you have accepted this as your only alternative, you should allow yourself the opportunity for some choices. It is ok to want the best for your child, after all doesn't everyone? So why is it wrong for you to want to provide your child with the chance for a better future—whether that is through the opportunity for advanced intelligence, increased drive, a charismatic personality, or a pleasing appearance?

Why, if you were an Ivy League graduate, is it wrong for you to prefer your genetic donor to be the same? Or, if you had always felt that you would have faired better in life if you were more outgoing, or were perhaps 3 inches taller, is it wrong to look for that in your donor? This should not be viewed as genetic manipulation or trying to produce a more perfect society. This is simply a parent wanting the best for their child and since the best would have been your own genes, then the next best should have some options along with it.

It is quite understandable that this is a very controversial subject and even the above stated will not be without its own share of attacks and reprisal. However, I feel extremely opinionated on this subject. I believe that just as we personally select our partners in life for procreation, we deserve the option to select the genetics that will replace ourselves or our loved one.

9. <u>What should we look for as standard medical or health criteria for a donor candidate?</u>

Most clinics do not recommend selecting a donor over the age of 33, due to the increased risk for chromosomal abnormalities in embryos of advanced maternal age. Our professional or personal recommendation is to not consider a donor over the age of 30, unless she has recently (within the past year) completed a prior donor cycle. While ASRM recommends working with donors over the age of 21, there are occasions when a donor over the age of 19 may be deemed appropriate, specifically if their current situation represents an increased maturity. It is also not recommended to accept any donor that has any family medical history of birth defects, mental disorders within the immediate family, genetic or chromosomal disorders. A donor's extensive family health history should be evaluated and accepted by a physician within the field of assisted reproduction, and under many circumstances, it is recommended that a genetic risk assessment be performed by a physician geneticist or genetics counselor. Before proceeding with an IVF cycle, all donors must undergo a complete medical and physical examination, psychological screening, and laboratory screening for sexually transmitted diseases.

10. <u>What are some of the expected fees involved with surrogacy and/or egg donation?</u>

Please contact your physician and a number of surrogacy and egg donor agencies directly for a comprehensive breakdown of expected costs. Please understand that the fees generally listed are estimates only. Be careful to always inquire about hidden costs or additional potential expenses along the way. While it is impossible to determine the exact cost of your specific situation, you should have a clear idea of what could potentially arise in a worse-case scenario situation. Fees listed by many agencies for outside professionals are often manipulated to appear that working through their office will be less costly so please inquire with each individual professional for their quoted rates. Be sure to factor in the costs for laboratory fees, consultation appointments, legal fees, donor and surrogate compensation, agency fees, psychological screening and counseling, fertility professional fees, insurance premiums and deductibles, travel costs, and miscellaneous expenses possibly incurred by the donor or throughout the pregnancy for the surrogate.

11. <u>Where should I begin with locating a donor?</u>

Most parents prefer to locate their donor through the assistance of their health care professional or through the services of an outside agency. The difference between these two options lies primarily in selection and wait time. Because most fertility centers offer donors only a very specific compensation, it limits the number of applicants available to provide to their patients, thereby increasing the wait time for parents through their office. The upside to this is the cap that is placed on a donor's compensation through a clinic is often more appealing to many couples, especially when considering the medical costs associated with IVF. Independent agencies vary in the compensation allowed to their donors, however, because they are in the business of advertising and screening donors, their primary focus is to locate and provide donors to parents. This leads to an increased number of candidates in many agency donor databases and often virtually no waiting list.

Still other parents are fortunate enough to locate their donor through the assistance of family or friends. This is a wonderful option for many parents, especially considering the fact that family health history and characteristics are known from the beginning. The downside to this option for many parents is the concern for potential confusion later in life. Often an open donor relationship is not appealing for the fear of mixed feelings on behalf of the donor once they child is born.

There are other avenues for locating a donor, be it through a personal advertisement or recommendation of a friend. Whatever the decision, be sure to have all of your information gathered before beginning the process, as locating a donor without the assistance of an agency or physician can be much more time consuming and disappointing than initially anticipated. Agencies have incorporated questionnaires, interview techniques, psychological evaluations and background investigations throughout their years of experience that is often well worth the added expense when considering selecting a donor. Selecting the genetics of your child is not something that you want to err on in any way. Being careful and smart, while keeping costs down is a balancing act that does require research and time, but in the end is worth every minute and every penny.

Abbreviations

Master Your New Language

AF—Aunt Flo or Menstrual Cycle

AI—Artificial Insemination

AID—Artificial Insemination by donor

AIH—Artificial Insemination by Husband

ART—Assisted Reproductive Technologies

ASRM—American Society for Reproductive Medicine

BBT—Basal Body Temperature

BCP—Birth Control Pills

D&C—Dilation & Curettage

DE—Donor Eggs

DES—Diethylstilbestrol (a synthetic estrogen)

DI—Donor Insemination

E2—Estradiol

FSH—Follicle Stimulating Hormone

ET—Embryo Transfer

FE—Frozen Embryo

FET—Frozen Embryo Transfer

FSH—Follicle Stimulating Hormone

GIFT—Gamete Intrafallopian Transfer

GnRH—Gonadotropin—Releasing Hormone

GS—Gestational Surrogate

HCG—Human Chorionic Gonadotropin

ICA—Injection of sperm into the cervical canal

ICSI—Intracytoplasmic Sperm Injection

IF—Intended Father

IM—Intended Mother

IP—Intended Parent

IUI—Intrauterine Insemination

IVF—In Vitro Fertilization

LH—Luteinizing Hormone

OHSS—Ovarian Hyperstimulation Syndrome

PCOS—Polycystic Ovarian Syndrome

PG—Pregnant

PMS—Pre-Menstrual Syndrome

RE—Reproductive Endocrinologist (Fertility Doctor)

SA—Semen Analysis

SART—Society for Assisted Reproduction Technology

SM—Surrogate Mother

STD—Sexually Transmitted Disease

TID—Therapeutic Insemination

TS—Traditional Surrogate

TSH—Thyroid Stimulating Hormone

US—Ultra Sound

ZIFT—Zygotte Intrafallopian Transfer

Glossary

Amniocentesis—A diagnostic procedure performed by inserting a hollow needle through the abdominal wall into the uterus and withdrawing a small amount of amniotic fluid from the sac surrounding the fetus. The amniotic fluid contains fetal cells and their DNA which can be analyzed to detect chromosome abnormalities, specific gene mutations, or certain birth defects.

Assisted Reproductive Technology (ART)—assisted reproductive technology (ART);—Catch-all phrase encompassing the use of medical assistance to treat infertility.

Artificial Insemination by Donor (AID)—Legal term for sperm donation. Medical community does not use word artificial but refers to this as therapeutic insemination (TID). If from the husband this is AIH.

Basal Body Temperature—Taking oral temperature to chart ovulation

Blastocyst—An embryo that has developed to the 128 cell stage, about the fifth day of development. Typically the cells are compacted and begin to differentiate into what will later become the baby and the placenta.

chorionic villus sampling (CVS)—Genetic analysis conducted using microscopic and other laboratory techniques to visualize and analyze chromosomes.

Collaborative Reproduction—Involvement of third parties in reproduction by persons who do not intend to raise the child assisted to be created.

Cryobank—A place which stores tissues for preserved by freezing

Cryopreservation—Deep freeze process used to store extra embryos or to store sperm for later use

Donor Egg—Egg donation from one woman usually combined with husband's sperm creating an embryo

Egg or Oocyte Transfer—Transfer of retrieved eggs into fallopian tubes through laparoscopy.

Embryo—Fertilized egg that has undergone one or more divisions; the production of axes of asymmetry in a developing embryo or tissue primordium.

Embryo Adoption—Term used f or individuals who offer their embryo(s) to another woman for implantation

Embryo Donor—Fertilized egg donated to another for implantation

Endometrium—Mucus membrane lining the uterus

Fertility—The ability to conceive

Fertility Drugs—Medication used to induce ovulation which can be prescribed by any physician. Clomid, Pergonal, Metrodin, Fertinez, Gonal-F or Folllistim.

Fetus—Unborn baby from the eighth week of pregnancy to birth.

Follicle—A part of the ovary containing a developing egg.

Follicle Stimulating Hormone—Produced by the pituitary gland and stimulates the ovary to allow ovulation. In men, stimulates the production of sperm in the testicles.

Gametes—Reproductive cells, sperm from men and eggs or oocytes from women.

Gamete Donation—In collaborative reproduction, donation of either sperm from men or eggs from women.

Gamete Intrafalllopian Transfer—Eggs and sperms place in the fallopian tube.

Gestation—Fetal development in the womb from conception to birth.

Gestational Carrier (formerly called gestational surrogate)—A woman who acts as a "host uterus" for a fetus not genetically related to her and, at birth, has a contractual obligation to release the child to the genetic parents.

Genetic Father—Man who supplies the sperm for the embryo

Genetic Mother—Woman who supplies the egg for the embryo

Hyperstimulation—Excessive stimulation of the ovaries to produce eggs which may cause the ovaries to become enlarged

Hysterectomy—Surgical removal of the uterus

Hysterosalpingogram—X-ray of the uterus and fallopian tubes

Infertility—Difficulty conceiving; defined as the failure to conceive despite unprotected intercourse after 6–12 months.

Implantation—Placing a fertilized egg in the endometrium of the uterus

Intended Parent—Man or woman who wants to have a child

Intracervical Insemination—Injection of sperm sample into the cervical canal

Intractyoplasmic sperm injection—Treatment for male infertility where a single sperm is injected directly into an egg.

Intrauterine insemination—Current, preferred medical term in lieu of "artificial" in which the washed sperm is inserted into the uterine cavity

In Vitro Fertilization—An ART procedure of removing eggs from ovaries and fertilizing with sperm in petri dish. Fertilization takes place outside a woman's body and embryos are transferred into woman's uterus

Laparoscopy—A surgical procedure in which a fiber optic instrument (a laparoscope) is inserted through a small incision in the abdomen to view the inside of the pelvis

Male Factor—Any cause of infertility due to sperm deficiencies or other male factors which make it difficult for the sperm to fertilize an egg under normal circumstances.

Miscarriage—Spontaneous abortion

Multifetal pregnancy reduction—Procedure to decrease the number of fetuses and improve the chances of the remaining fetuses to be carried to term.

Multiple birth—A pregnancy with multiple fetuses.

Multiple gestation—A pregnancy with multiple fetuses.

Oligospermia—Abnormally low number of sperm in the male ejaculate

Oocyte (Ovum)—Egg (reproductive cell) produced in the ovaries.

Oocyte Retrieval—Surgical procedure to collect eggs in the ovarian follicles

Ovarian monitoring—Use of ultrasound, blood and/or urine tests to monitor follicle development and hormone production.

Ovulatory Dysfunction—A cause of infertility due to problems with egg production by the ovaries.

Ovaries—Sexual glands of the female where ova develop and which produce the hormones estrogen and progesterone

Ovulation—Release of ripened egg from its follicle in the ovary

Pregnancy (clinical)—Documentation of pregnancy by a presence of a gestational sac. For ART data collection, pregnancy is a clinical pregnancy versus a chemical (positive pregnancy test) pregnancy.

Primary Infertility—Infertility with persons who have never given birth.

Reproductive Endocrinologist—An ob-gyn whose specialty is the treatment of hormonal disorders that affect reproductive function

Reproductive Surgeon—Physician, ob-gyn or urologist whose specialty is correcting impaired reproductive functions

Secondary Infertility—Infertility in individuals who have already given birth.

Semen—Seminal fluid and sperm ejaculated during orgasm

Semen Analysis—The examination and analysis of a semen specimen for sperm count, motility, and morphology

Sperm—The male reproductive cell.

Sperm Buffer—A fresh semen specimen is collected f or cold shipping and ultimate insemination

Sperm Count—Also called sperm density—the number of sperm per milliliter of semen. Norman sperm count is twenty million or more per milliliter.

Sperm Morphology—The analysis of the form and structure of sperm

Sperm Motility—The analysis of the percentage of mobile sperm in a semen sample—fifty percent or more is normally moving rapidly

Sperm Washing—A technique that separate sperm from the seminal fluid

Stimulated Cycle—An ART cycle in which a woman receives oral or injected fertility drugs to stimulate her ovaries to produce more follicles.

Surrogate—A woman who agrees to bear a child f or another individual or couple. Term has evolved to mean those pregnancies where the woman contributes her own genetic material and gestates the child.

Thawed Cycle—A cycle in which frozen embryos are thawed for transfer.

Tubal Factor—One or both fallopian tubes have structural or functional dysfunction reducing fertility.

Unexplained Cause of Infertility—After a comprehensive evaluation there is no cause for infertility.

Unstimulated Cycle—An ART cycle in which the woman does not receive fertility drugs but the follicles are allowed to develop naturally.

Urologist—A physician who specializes in the surgical treatment of disorders of the urinary tract and male reproductive tract.

Zonapellucida—The protective coating surrounding the egg

Zygote—An egg that has been fertilized but not yet divided

Zygote Intra Fallopian Transfer (ZIFT)—Transfer of the zygote into the fallopian tube during in vitro fertilization

Resources

American Infertility Association
666 Fifth Avenue, Suite 278
New York, NY 10103
(718) 621-5083
www.americaninfertility.org
info@americanfertility.org

American Society for Reproductive Medicine
1209 Montgomery Highway
Birmingham, AL 35216-2809
(205) 978-5000
www.asrm.org

Resolve
1310 Broadway
Somerville, MA 02144
(617) 623-0744
www.Resolve.org
info@resolve.org

The Society for Assisted Reproductive Technology
Joyce Zeitz, Executive Administrator
1209 Montgomery Highway
Birmingham, AL 35216
(205) 978-5000 X109
www.sart.com
jzeitz@asrm.org

Adoptive Breastfeeding

The Newman-Goldfarb Induced Lactation Protocol and general information
www.asklenore.com/

Breastfeeding the Adopted Baby, rev. ed.
Debra Stewart Peterson, Corona © 1994

The American Surrogacy Center
(surrogacy and egg donor information)
www.surrogacy.com

Child of My Dreams: Adoption and Infertility Support
www.childofmydreams.com

National Embryo Donation Center
www.embryodonation.org

Additional Embryo Donation Sites:
www.CenterforHumanReprod.com
www.resolve.org
www.embryosalive.com
www.cdc.gov
www.embryoptions.com
www.embryodonation.org

Intended Parents. Com
www.intendedparents.com

La leche League
www.laleche.org

Offspring: for children seeking sperm donor parents
www.cbc.ca/programs/sites/features/offspring/index.htm

Online Infertility Support Groups
www.surrogacy.com/group/ogroups.html

Sperm Bank Directory
www.spermbankdirectory.com

Sperm Bank List
www.fertilityplus.org/faq/donor.html#sperm

Surrogate Mothers Online
www.surromomsonline.com

Gay & Lesbian Parenting
www.familieslikeours.org
www.familypride.org
www.gayfamilyoptions.com
www.geocities.com/gayparenting
www.haydennet.com/parenting
www.lesbian.org/lesbian-moms/index.html
www.ourfamily.org
www.proudparenting.com
www.queerparents.org
www.colage.org—a group called Children of Lesbians and Gays Everywhere—a national support group that gives children a safe place to share their experiences.
www.cyrobank.com
www.fairfaxcryobank.com
www.pacrepro.com
www.gayspermbank.com
www.thespermbankofca.org
www.xytex.com

Gestational Surrogacy
A Matter of Trust: The Guide to Gestational Surrogacy
Gail Dutton
Clouds Publishing ©1997

Embryo Donation
The long Awaited Stork: A Guide to Parenting After Infertility
Ellen Sarasohn Glazer
Jossey-Bass ©1998

Additional Infertility Titles:

Alternative Beginnings: A Woman's Guide to Getting Pregnant by Self-Insemination
By Lisa Saffron

Choosing Assisted Reproduction: Social, Emotional & Ethical Considerations
By Susan Cooper

Choosing to Be Open about Donor Conception
By Sharon Pettle and Ian Burns

Having a Baby Without a Man: The Woman's Guide to Alternative Insemination
By Susan Robinson, M.D. and H.F. Pizer, P.A.C.

Helping the Stork: The Choices and Challenges of Donor Insemination
By Carol Frost Vercollone, et al

Taking Charge of Infertility
By Patricia Irwin Johnston

How Babies and Families Are Made: There Is More Than One Way!
By Patricia Shaffer

How I Began: The Story of Donor Insemination
By Julia Paul

Let Me Explain: A Story About Donor Insemination
By Jane Schnitter

Mommy Did I Grow in Your Tummy? Where Some Babies Come From
By Elaine R. Gordon

Phoebe's Family: A Story about Egg Donation
By Linda Stamm

Appendix A

Sample Surrogacy Agreement Provisions

The following provisions are essential in each surrogacy agreement:

INTRODUCTION OF PARTIES—all parties involved must be declared, to include the husband of the egg donor if applicable.

1. PURPOSE AND INTENT OF PARTIES

2. REPRESENTATIONS AND WARRANTIES

3. NO WARRANTIES OR GUARANTIES BY PROFESSIONALS

4. CUSTODY AND PARENTAL RIGHTS—this is a relinquishment of all parental rights by the surrogate donor (and her spouse, if any) whereby she is not responsible for the rearing of any resulting child.

5. MEDICAL AND PSYCHOLOGICAL EVALUATIONS AND SCREENINGS

6. GENERAL TRANSFER PROCEDURE

7. ASSUMPTION OF MEDICAL RISKS AND RELEASE—there is an inherent risk in any medical procedure, and the parties must specifically assume any non-negligently inflicted injury.

8. SURROGATE'S CONDUCT

9. ABORTION, MISCARRIAGE, AND SELECTIVE TERMINATION—due to <u>Roe V. Wade</u>, a woman has the fundamental right to privacy governing

her ability to control her reproductive freedom, and more specifically, her pregnancy. And, since the law has not developed any further in this area, this issue should be addressed fully.

10. COMPENSATION AND PAYMENT OF EXPENSES

11. MEDICAL INSURANCE

12. LIFE INSURANCE

13. TRUST ACCOUNT

14. FACILITATION OF LEGAL PROCESSES

15. NAME OF CHILD

16. FUTURE CONTACT—do the parties want or expect contact in the future, to include pictures, phone calls, or contact for medical reasons.

17. PRIVACY AND CONFIDENTIALITY

18. CHANGES IN CIRCUMSTANCE

19. DEATH OR DIVORCE OF INTENDED PARENTS

20. INDEPENDENT LEGAL COUNSEL—so that there is not an issue later as to whether there was a "meeting of the minds," each party must have their own counsel.

21. CONFIRMATION OF GENETIC PARENTAGE

22. BREACH

23. ASSUMPTION OF RISKS OF ABNORMAL CHILD/GENDER OF CHILD

24. LIFE SUPPORT

25. RESPONSIBILITIES IN THE EVENT OF STILLBIRTH OR MISCARRIAGE

26. TERMINATION OF AGREEMENT—this informs the parties as to when and under what circumstances the agreement may be terminated.

27. DISPUTE RESOLUTION/ARBITRATION

28. INTENTION OF THE PARTIES

29. AGENCY, PARTNERSHIP, EMPLOYMENT OR JOINT VENTURE

30. SELECTION OF SURROGATE MADE WITHOUT RECOMMENDATION OF COUNSEL

31. TAXATION AND IMMIGRATION

32. WRITTEN AGREEMENT

33. EXECUTION OF AGREEMENT

34. ENTIRE AGREEMENT, INTEGRATION AND ENUREMENT

35. INTERPRETATION

36. ENFORCEABILITY OF AGREEMENT

37. EXECUTION OF AGREEMENT

38. GOVERNING LAW—which jurisdiction's laws will apply?

39. SURVIVAL—certain terms in the agreement must continue beyond the length of this actual agreement; therefore, this section will describe those areas to the parties.

40. ACKNOWLEDGMENTS & SIGNATURES OF THE PARTIES

EXHIBIT "A" (PAYMENT SCHEDULE AND ADDITIONAL CONSIDERATION)

MEDICAL AUTHORIZATION OF SURROGATE

Appendix B

Sample Egg Donor Agreement Provisions

The following provisions are essential in each donor agreement:

INTRODUCTION OF PARTIES—all parties involved must be declared, to include the husband of the egg donor if applicable.

1. PURPOSE AND INTENT OF PARTIES AND AGREEMENT

2. REPRESENTATIONS AND WARRANTIES

3. NO WARRANTIES OR GUARANTIES BY PROFESSIONALS

4. PARENTAL RIGHTS AND RESPONSIBILITIES—this is a relinquishment of all parental rights by the donor (and her spouse, if any) whereby she is not responsible for the rearing of any resulting child.

5. EGG RETRIEVAL AND DONATION—this section informs the parties of the procedures that are to be undertaken in order to complete an egg donation.

6. MEDICAL AND PSYCHOLOGICAL EVALUATIONS AND SCREEN-INGS

7. ASSUMPTION OF MEDICAL AND PSYCHOLOGICAL RISKS—there is an inherent risk in any medical procedure, and the parties must specifically assume any non-negligently inflicted injury.

8. EGG DONOR'S CONDUCT—this informs the donor of the protocol that she must follow from the treating IVF physician.

9. CONSIDERATION—what will the donor receive in exchange for her pain and suffering?

10. PAYMENT OF MEDICAL EXPENSES—who is responsible for all medical expenses?

11. MEDICAL INSURANCE—the donor must be protected by a catastrophic policy despite any personal insurance that she holds.

12. PRIVACY AND CONFIDENTIALITY

13. DEATH, SEPARATION OR DIVORCE OF INTENDED PARENTS— this section informs the parties of the disposition of the embryos in the event of the above listed events. It is also important for the donor to be aware of what the intended parents intend to do with the embryos once they have completed their family, such as donation to other couples, donation to science and research, or destruction by thawing.

14. FUTURE CONTACT—do the parties want or expect contact in the future, to include pictures, phone calls, or contact for medical reasons.

15. INDEPENDENT LEGAL COUNSEL—each party to the agreement should have their own attorney.

16. CHANGES IN CIRCUMSTANCE

17. EXCHANGE OF INFORMATION—this is similar to number 14 above.

18. ANONYMITY—this applies if the parties intend to remain anonymous.

19. TERMINATION OF THIS AGREEMENT—this informs the parties as to when and under what circumstances the agreement may be terminated.

20. BREACH

21. TIME OF THE ESSENCE

22. DISPUTE RESOLUTION

23. NO AGENCY, PARTNERSHIP, EMPLOYMENT OR JOINT VENTURE

24. ATTORNEYS FEES AND COSTS

25. TAXATION

26. WRITTEN AGREEMENT

27. EXECUTION OF AGREEMENT

28. ENTIRE AGREEMENT AND INUREMENT

29. INTERPRETATION

30. ENFORCEABILITY OF AGREEMENT

31. EXECUTION OF AGREEMENT

32. GOVERNING LAW—which jurisdiction's laws will apply?

33. CONFLICTING MEDICAL FORMS—the parties must be aware that they may be presented with medical forms that do not apply to their particular situation and/or status. In that case, the parties need to be aware that they must no answer these questions.

34. SURVIVAL—certain terms in the agreement must continue beyond the length of this actual agreement; therefore, this section will describe those areas to the parties.

35. ACKNOWLEDGMENTS & SIGNATURES OF THE PARTIES

Appendix C

Sample Embryo Donation Agreement Provisions

The following provisions are essential in each embryo donor agreement:

INTRODUCTION OF PARTIES—all parties involved must be declared, to include the husband of the egg donor if applicable.

1. PURPOSE AND INTENT OF PARTIES AND AGREEMENT

2. REPRESENTATIONS AND WARRANTIES

3. NO WARRANTIES OR GUARANTIES BY PROFESSIONALS

4. PARENTAL RIGHTS AND RESPONSIBILITIES—this is a relinquishment of all parental rights by the donor (and her spouse, if any) whereby she is not responsible for the rearing of any resulting child.

5. THE EMBRYO DONATION

6. EXTINGUISHMENT OF LEGAL RIGHTS AND RESPONSIBILITIES OF EMBRYO DONORS

7. RELEASE AND INDEMNIFICATION

8. TRANSFER OF POSSESSION OF EMBRYOS FROM MEDICAL FACILITY

9. PSYCHOLOGICAL EVALUATIONS AND SCREENINGS

10. ASSUMPTION OF MEDICAL AND PSYCHOLOGICAL RISKS

11. CONSIDERATION

12. PRIVACY AND CONFIDENTIALITY

13. FUTURE CONTACT—do the parties want or expect contact in the future, to include pictures, phone calls, or contact for medical reasons.

14. CHANGE OF ADDRESS

15. INDEPENDENT LEGAL COUNSEL—each party to the agreement should have their own attorney.

16. BREACH

17. TIME OF THE ESSENCE

18. DISPUTE RESOLUTION

19. NO AGENCY, PARTNERSHIP, EMPLOYMENT OR JOINT VEN-TURE

20. ATTORNEYS FEES AND COSTS

21. TAXATION

22. WRITTEN AGREEMENT

23. EXECUTION OF AGREEMENT

24. ENTIRE AGREEMENT AND INUREMENT

25. INTERPRETATION

26. ENFORCEABILITY OF AGREEMENT

27. EXECUTION OF AGREEMENT

28. GOVERNING LAW—which jurisdiction's law will apply?

29. SURVIVAL—certain terms in the agreement must continue beyond the length of this actual agreement; therefore, this section will describe those areas to the parties.

30. ACKNOWLEDGMENTS & SIGNATURES OF THE PARTIES

Note: this information is an attempt to provide guidance regarding the important issues that egg donors, surrogates, embryo donors, sperm donors and Intended Parents should consider prior to entering into any agreement. This is not meant to replace representation by and consultation with medical professionals, mental health counselors or lawyers handling these arrangements. The serious nature of the legal rights of the parties in these agreements necessitates careful research and consideration prior to entering into any agreement. A carefully drafted agreement must detail consents and should outline the issues involved. Furthermore, the agreement must delineate the rights and responsibilities of all parties to the agreement. It is only through this process that the parties can be confident that a child born through third party assisted reproduction is free from legal conflict.

Appendix D

History of Reproductive Technologies—This Has Been Going On for How Long?

New biotechnologies are providing the human race with new capacities for altering human reproduction. However, many groups are concerned with reproductive technologies going in the wrong direction—or in a direction that threatens the human race as we know it. Fortunately, you can rest assured, because that is not the case. Third party assisted reproduction, although cutting edge, has been helping couples and individuals have children when the possibility may not have existed for them before.

It all began in 1790 when the world experienced the first successful case of human artificial insemination, although most of the world probably did not know it. Some additional dates worth mentioning are as follows:

1884—First artificial insemination using donor sperm; U.S. doctor William Pancoast inseminates a patient with sperm from one of his students

1944—First successful in vitro fertilization (IVF) of a human egg

1954—First successful pregnancy using frozen sperm

1968—Robert Edwards and co-workers in Britain fertilize human eggs in a test tube

1975—First successful IVF pregnancy achieved, although no birth resulted

1978—Louis Brown, the first IVF (test-tube) baby is born in England

1981—Elizabeth Jordan Carr, the first American baby to be conceived by IVF, baby is born in Norfolk, Virginia

1984—First baby born from a frozen embryo, Zoe Leyland, in Australia

1990—First unaffected child is born following PGD—originally developed as an alternative to prenatal diagnosis for those with an increased risk of transmitting a single gene or chromosomal abnormality to their offspring, although more recently it has been used in conjunction with certain IVF patients with the goal of increasing IVF success rates. In fact, at these early stages, PGD still has many issues surrounding its use. For example, should a couple choose to use PGD because of improved technologies and standard of care, for fear of the liability to our children born with discoverable diseases, or because of a duty to inform IVF patients of its availability? Or, can we use it for family balancing, avoiding gender-linked diseases, aiding an ailing child or relative, or even genetic enhancements?

1992—First successful pregnancy using ICSI (Intracytoplasmic Sperm Injection)

1966—A 63 year old Southern California woman gives birth to a baby using a donated egg

1997—First successful birth using frozen eggs

1999—Natalie Brown, younger sister of Louise Brown, becomes the first test tube baby to naturally give birth to a child

2003—65 year old becomes the oldest known woman in the world to give birth using eggs from her niece and sperm from her niece's husband[26]

2003—More than 1 million babies have been born using in vitro fertilization, including more than 200,000 in the United States[27]

Now, with all of this technology available worldwide, there have been approximately one million babies born as a result of IVF worldwide. In the United States in 2000, there were 35,025 babies born as a result of IVF, GIFT or ZIFT (which only makes up about 1% of all births in the United States itself). Furthermore, more than 4000 PGD cycles have been performed worldwide as of April of 2002, with more than 1000 babies born as a result of IVF-PGD procedures.[28]

---

26. http://www.dnapolicy.org/genetics/chronology.jhtml

27. American Society for Reproductive Medicine and U.S. Centers for Disease Control and Prevention

28. http://www.dnapolicy.org/genetics/facts.jhtml

Table of Authorities

CASES

STATUTES

OTHER AUTHORITIES

Index

About the Authors

THERESA ERICKSON—SHE IS AVAILABLE FOR CONSULTATION BY GOING TO HER WEBSITE AT WWW.SURROGACYLAWYER.NET. IN ADDITION, SHE IS AVAILABLE VIA WWW.INCIID.ORG WHERE SHE IS AN ONLINE MODERATOR FOR THE LEGAL ISSUES REGARDING EGG DONATION, SURROGACY, EMBRYO DONATION AND OTHER SIMILAR ISSUES.

MARYANN LATHUS—SHE IS AVAILABLE FOR CONSULTATION BY GOING TO WWW.CONCEPTUALOPTIONS.COM.

0-595-34319-8